Sewn Bags

STYLISH BAGS FOR EVERY OCCASION

Sewn Bags

STYLISH BAGS FOR EVERY OCCASION

THE GUILD OF MASTER CRAFTSMAN PUBLICATIONS

First published 2016 by
Guild of Master Craftsman Publications Ltd
Castle Place, 166 High Street, Lewes,
East Sussex, BN7 1XU

All projects first published in *Making* magazine

ISBN 978 1 78494 171 0

Publisher: Jonathan Bailey
Production Manager: Jim Bulley
Senior Project Editor: Dominique Page
Designer: Ginny Zeal
Illustrators: Vicky Woodgate, Sarah Skeate and Emma Cowley
Photographers: Laurel Guilfoyle, Pete Jones and Emma Noren

Set in Akidenz Grotesk and Grand Hotel Regular

Colour origination by GMC Reprographics
Printed and bound in Malaysia

Credits
(p.9) project designer: Sue Bower; (p.13) project designer:
Emma Brennan; (p.17) project designer and step
photography: Emma Brennan; (p.23) project designer and
step photography: Emma Brennan; (p.29) project designer:
Suzanne Rowland; step photography: Ben Rowland; (p.33)
project designer: Emma Herian; (p.37) project designer:
Suzanne Rowland; (p.41) project designer: Suzanne Rowland;
(p.45) project designer and step photography: Suzanne
Rowland; (p.49) project designer: Suzanne Rowland; (p.53)
project designer and step photography: Jemima Schlee;
(p.57) project designer and step photography: Jemima
Schlee; (p.61) project designer and step photography:
Jemima Schlee; (p.67) project designer and step
photography: Jemima Schlee; (p.73) project designer and
step photography: Jemima Schlee; (p.79) project designer:
Vanessa Mooncie; (p.83) project designer and step
photography: Vanessa Mooncie; (p.89) project designer and
step photography: Jemima Schlee; (p.95) project designer
and step photography: Emma Herian; (p.99) project designer:
Diana Uprichard.

Contents

Introduction

As we all know, you can never have enough bags. This book brings together a stylish collection of 20 easy-to-make, sewn bags by a selection of experienced designers and makers. Suitable for an array of different occasions, there's something for everyone. You can have fun choosing fabrics and embellishments to complement your outfits, or enjoy making the projects as gifts for friends and family.

Sewing is undoubtedly one of the most rewarding hobbies you can have, and a fun and easy one to learn. With clear text, photographs, detailed illustrations and templates, most of the projects in this book are suitable for those new to sewing. If you are a novice, then we recommend you begin by making some of the bags exactly as they are shown, so that you can build your skill level. Once you feel more confident, you can move on to using the projects as design inspiration, and change a few things to make them your own. You may also find you like parts of two different projects, and you can mix them together to produce your own unique bag.

With so many designs to choose from, this book is the perfect place to indulge in a serious love of bags. So, grab your favourite stash of fabrics and your sewing machine, and get started – you'll soon have a beautiful, bespoke bag to swing on your arm and admire.

Summer Bag

This pretty fabric bag is the perfect accessory for relaxed summer style. It is ideal for collecting your shopping from the local deli, carrying a book and sandwich to the park or your swimming costume and towel to the beach.

You will need:

- 20in (50cm) each of 2 contrasting fabrics, 60in (1.5m) wide, for bag
- 20in (50cm) of another contrasting fabric, 60in (1.5m) wide, for binding and handles
- 20in (50cm) calico for lining (or a fabric of your choice)
- Thread to match fabric
- Sewing machine
- Iron and ironing board
- Tape measure
- Fabric scissors and pins
- Needle

1 From the main bag fabrics cut two pieces 8 x 23⅝in (20 x 61cm) from each of the two contrasting fabrics. Lay out the fabrics as shown in the diagram on page 11. With right sides together, machine stitch the bottom of one oblong to the bottom side of a contrasting oblong, stopping ⅜in (1cm) from the right-hand side of each piece. Join the two 'L' shapes, right sides together, matching the seams in the centre as shown in the diagram.

2 Press all the seams open with a warm iron. Make up the lining fabric in the same way, but reversing the shape so that the lining will lay on top of the bag with wrong sides facing. Pin the main bag to the lining to hold it in place.

3 Cut four strips of the binding fabric 2 x 27½in (5 x 70cm). Fold each strip in half lengthways and press. Attach one bias strip, raw edges together, to the 8in (20cm) end of each long panel. Stop stitching ⅜in (1cm) from the right-hand side (see diagram). Fold the binding over to the lining side and slipstitch in place, stopping ⅜in (1cm) from the right-hand side.

Tips

This bag can be washed if you pre-shrink your fabric before stitching.

Linen-weight fabric will help the bag keep its shape.

4 With right sides together, stitch each long side to a short side (see arrows on diagram). You will have a length of fabric left over. Don't worry about this, as it will form the point for the handles.

5 Bring the bias binding down each of the raw edge sides of the bag and machine with right sides together covering the whole length of the raw edge (approx. 23in/58cm). Fold over the binding and slipstitch to the lining side. This will enclose all the raw edges and makes a neat finish to the inside of the bag.

6 Make the handles by cutting two strips of the handle fabric 5⅛ x 38in (13 x 97cm). Fold in half lengthways and press. Open out and fold in each side of the length to the centre, press, then fold in half again and press once more. Machine stitch along the length of the handle ⅜in (1cm) from each side so that you have two lines of stitching. This will reinforce the handle and help keep its shape.

7 Attach the handles by folding over 1³⁄₁₆in (2cm) at the end of each handle and stitch them in place, one at each point of the bag. Stitch over twice to ensure the handle is secure. You can stitch the handles to the inside or outside of the bag depending on your preference. Trim all threads.

How to lay out your fabric

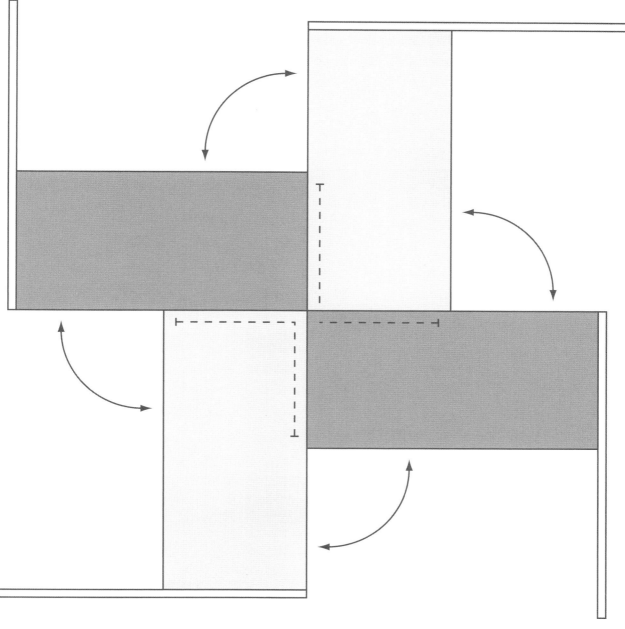

Bow-trimmed Clutch

The oversized bow turns this lovely clutch bag into a real statement piece, suitable for everything from days out to special summer evenings. Using just two pattern pieces, the pouch shape simply folds over at the top to form a flap.

You will need:

- Pattern templates on pages 102–103
- Photocopier
- 20in (50cm) of 45¼in (115cm) wide exterior fabric (cotton print, needlecord or similar)
- 15¾in (40cm) of 36¼in (92cm) wide lining fabric
- 15¾in (40cm) of 36¼in (92cm) wide interfacing
- Fusible web, 6 x 6in (15 x 15cm), for bow centre
- Magnetic snap
- Thread to match fabric
- Sewing machine
- Needle
- Iron, ironing board and handkerchief or pressing cloth
- Fabric scissors
- Pins

Tips

Use a soft fabric and wadding/quilted interfacing so that the bag has substance but is still soft enough to fold over easily.

You could make your bag in floral cotton fabrics with a contrasting bow for summer, or in velvet or silk brocade for evening wear.

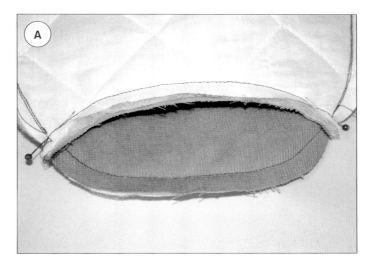

1 Enlarge the pattern templates as directed and cut out the pieces you need. Place a handkerchief or clean piece of cloth over the top and iron the fusible web to the back of the piece. Cut two bow pieces on fold from fabric.

2 Iron or sew interfacing to wrong side of bag front and back pieces. Also interface back lining if the fabric is lightweight. Transfer dots and snap marks from pattern to reverse/interfaced side of fabric. Fix magnetic half of snap to front at marker point.

3 With front and back pieces right sides together, stitch together round side and lower edges, stopping either side at dots marked on pattern pieces (see A).

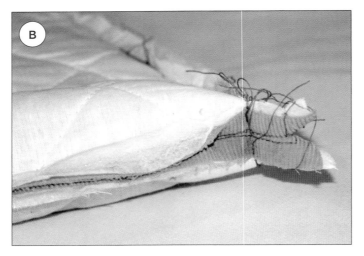

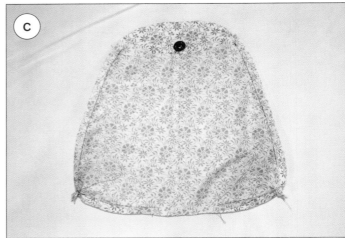

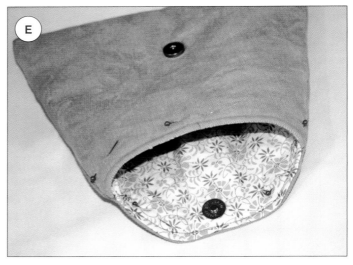

4 Insert a finger into one of the bottom corners. Match up seams on bottom and side, pin through all thicknesses and stitch straight across the corner to form a base for the bag (see B). Clip excess material from corner.

5 Iron interfacing to back lining and fix non-magnetic half of snap at point marked on template. Stitch lining front/back together and form box corners as you did for main bag pieces but remember to leave a gap of around 4in (10cm) at centre of bottom to turn the bag through (see C).

6 Insert bag into lining with right sides together. Pin lining and bag together at upper edges, with raw edges even. Stitch front edge, first stopping at dots/side seam. Then stitch back edge, again stopping at dots/side seam. Stitch through all thicknesses. Clip into seam allowance all round top edge to free up the curve (see D).

7 Turn bag through opening in lining and push lining to inside of bag. Roll lining with your fingers so that it is not visible from the outside and pin in place round top (see E). Topstitch through all layers, about ⅜in (1cm) from top edge of bag, using a long stitch length. Press well.

8 Slipstitch opening in lining closed and tuck lining back into bag. Fold top of bag over carefully and do up snap. Press bag well with snap fastened.

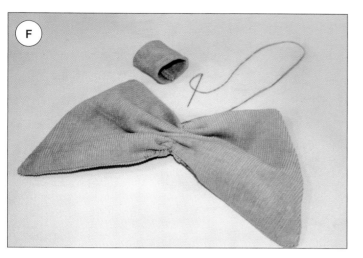

9 Make the bow using the bow and bow centre templates on page 103. Cut two bow pieces from your main fabric. Pin and stitch the two bow pieces with right sides together round the outside edge, leaving a ⅜in (1cm) seam allowance and a gap of about 1³⁄₁₆in (3cm) at the lower edge to turn the bow through. Clip seam allowance at corners. Turn bow right side out, slipstitch gap in seam and press. Run a gathering stitch up the centre of the turned bow and pull gathers up, securing the thread at one end (see F). Cover with a damp handkerchief or pressing cloth and iron fusible web to reverse of bow centre and fold in long edges marked with a dotted line on pattern template to the centre. Fuse in place. With right sides together and raw edges even, stitch two short ends together. Turn bow centre right side out. Feed gathered bow through bow centre, and make a few hand stitches to secure the bow in place.

10 Hand-stitch bow to bag flap centrally, so lower edge of bow centre is level with edge of folded over flap (see G).

Tips
The only tricky part of this project is sewing the lining and bag together. Make sure that you stitch the front and back sections together separately and only stitch to the dot marks/side seams on both sides.

If you prefer, add a sew-on snap to the bag once you have completed it.

Retro Handbag

Made in eye-catching Japanese Pop Art-style fabric and paired with a bright vinyl handle and two big plastic buttons, this bag takes you right back to the decade associated with the birth of British pop music and fashion – the 1960s.

You will need:

- Pattern templates on page 104
- Photocopier
- 27½in (70cm) of 44in (112cm) wide bright printed fabric, for bag exterior
- 27½in (70cm) of 44in (112cm) wide lining fabric, for bag lining and interior pocket
- 18in (45cm) of 36in (92cm) wide firm sew-in interfacing, for bag body
- 12in (30cm) of 36in (92cm) wide fusible interfacing, for flap
- 14 x 2in (36 x 5cm) piece of plastic canvas or similar, to stiffen bag base
- One vinyl or leather bag handle approx. 21½in (55cm) long
- One magnetic snap set
- Two big buttons (approx. 2in/5cm diameter)
- Optional extra snap and small button, for interior pocket
- Thread to match fabric
- Sewing machine
- Iron and ironing board
- Pins, needle, tape measure
- Fabric scissors

Note: The finished bag size is approximately 12in (30cm) high, by 15in (38cm) wide and 2in (5cm) at the base. Seams are ⅜in (1cm) unless otherwise stated.

1 Enlarge the pattern templates for bag front/back and flap. Then cut the relevant number of pieces as directed on each pattern template.

2 Pin the bag front and back sections to the corresponding front/back interfacing sections and baste together round the entire outside edge, about ⅜in (1cm) from the raw edge. Make sure the edges of the exterior fabric align with the edges of the interfacing (see A). Transfer the snap marker from the front/back pattern template and fix the magnetic half of the snap to the bag front.

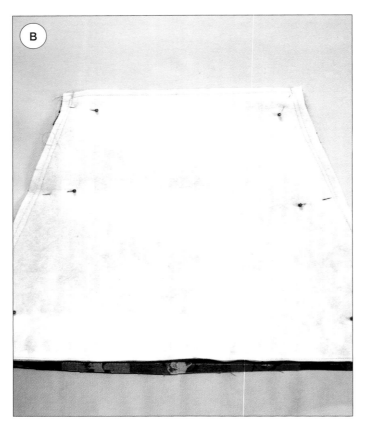

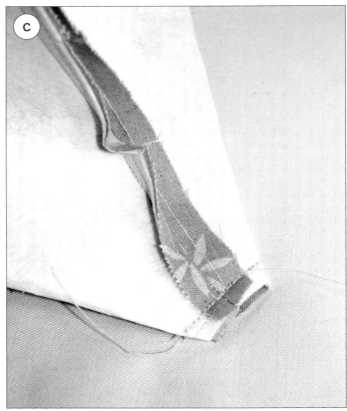

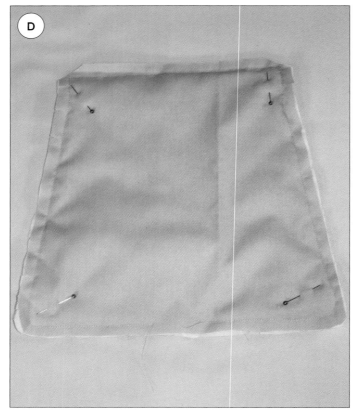

3 With right sides together pin interfaced front/back pieces. Stitch together at side and lower edges, leaving corners free (see B).

4 Fold lower corners of bag, matching centre of side seam with lower seam, and pin in place. Stitch straight across to form a flat base for the bag. Remove pins. Each corner seam will measure about 2in (5cm) across (see C). Clip side seam allowance both sides to free up the seam a little, turn bag right side out and press.

5 Iron interfacing to wrong side of both flap pieces. Transfer magnetic snap position mark from template onto flap underside and fix non-magnetic half of snap. Pin flap sections right sides together, stitch together round sides and lower edges. Clip into seam allowance at corners, turn flap right side out and press. Topstitch round flap about ⅜in (1cm) from the edge.

6 Mark centre of flap and bag back with pins. With centre points together, pin and stitch finished flap onto back of bag, right outside of flap against right outside of bag back, with raw edges even.

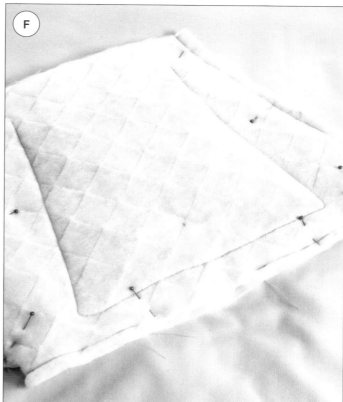

7 To make an interior pocket, cut two flap pieces on the fold from lining fabric. Pin pieces with right sides together and, leaving a gap in the seam at the lower edge of about 2½in (6cm) to turn pocket through, stitch together round outside edge, leaving a ⅜in (1cm) seam allowance. Clip seam at corners, turn pocket right side out through gap and press. Slipstitch gap closed and topstitch upper edge about ³⁄₁₆in (5mm) from the edge (see D).

8 Place interior pocket with right side uppermost onto right side of back lining. **Note:** Upper edge of pocket should be about 1½in (4cm) down from the top edge of bag back lining. Stitch in place around side and lower edges about ³⁄₁₆in (5mm) from the edge (see E).

9 Stitch front and back lining pieces with right sides together. Stitch at side and lower edges, leaving corners free. Leave a gap in the seam at the bottom of about 4¾in (12cm) for turning the bag through (see F). Fold the lower corners of the bag, matching seams, and stitch straight across to form a base for the bag lining as you did for main bag (see G).

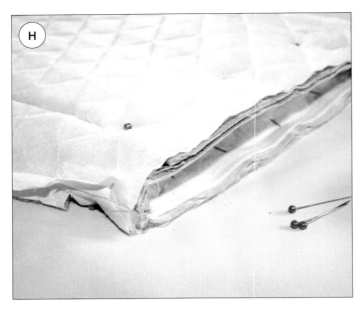

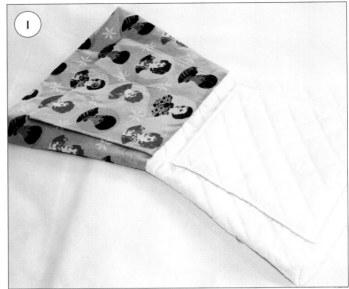

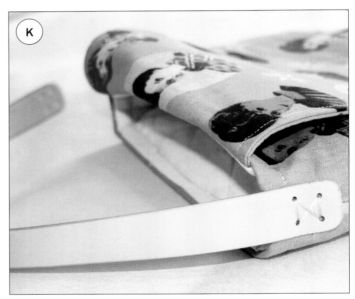

10 Insert bag into lining with right sides together and pin bag and lining together through all thicknesses round upper edges with raw edges even. **Note:** You will be pinning through the flap too. Stitch, leaving a seam allowance of about ⅝in (1.5cm). Clip into seam allowance at intervals all round (see H).

11 Turn bag right side out through opening in bottom of lining (see I) and push lining to inside of bag. Turn flap upwards and roll lining with your fingers so it is not visible from the outside and pin in place all round top. Topstitch through all layers, about ⅝in (1.5cm) from top of bag (see J).

12 Insert rectangle of plastic canvas in bag base through gap, slip-stitch gap closed, tuck lining back into bag and press.

13 Stitch handle to bag. The handle used here has pre-made holes for hand-sewing to the bag. Sew in a cross pattern for extra strength. The lower edge of the handle should be about 1⅜in (3.5cm) down from the finished upper edge and sit centrally over the side seam (see K). Sew through bag and lining.

14 Stitch the two big buttons centrally on the flap, above each
other and about 2½in (6cm) apart (see L). If you like, you can also
stitch a snap to the centre of the interior pocket to make it more
secure. Finish with another button for decoration.

Messenger Bag

The clean, modern lines of this simple tweed bag make it an invaluable addition to a gent's winter wardrobe. Big enough to house a laptop or documents, it's a versatile-sized bag with a contemporary edge.

You will need:

- Pattern templates on pages 105–106
- Photocopier
- 30in (75cm) of 60in (154cm) wide Harris Tweed, or similar
- 31½in (80cm) of 36in (92cm) wide firm or craft-weight sew-in interfacing, for bag body (plus optional same of wadding to give extra body)
- 24in (60cm) of 36in (92cm) wide fusible interfacing, for flap and pockets
- 28in (70cm) of 45in (114cm) wide lining fabric, for bag body and pocket linings (quilted fabric adds substance)
- 21in (53cm) of 1in (2.5cm) wide nylon webbing tape, for fastener (cut into 7in (18cm) and 14in (35cm) lengths)
- 1in (2.5cm) wide plastic two-part fastener
- 61in (155cm) of 2in (5cm) wide nylon webbing tape, for strap (cut into two 6in (15cm) lengths and one 49in (125cm) length
- Two metal or plastic rectangular-shaped O-rings, 2in (5cm) wide
- One 2in (5cm) wide plastic 'slider' buckle to match webbing
- 2¾ x 14in (7 x 36cm) piece of plastic canvas or thick craft interfacing, for bag base
- One piece of ¾ x 2in (2 x 5cm) Velcro/riptape
- Three buttons, 1in (2.5cm) diameter
- Thread to match fabric
- Sewing machine
- Iron, ironing board and handkerchief or pressing cloth
- Fabric scissors
- Pins and needle

Note: All seam allowances have been included on the template and are ⅜in (1cm) unless otherwise stated.

1 Start by copying the templates at the correct size. Then cut out the relevant number of pieces in fabric, interfacing and lining as directed on each pattern template.

2 To make exterior and interior pockets, place a handkerchief or pressing cloth over the top and iron the fusible interfacing to the wrong side of the pocket pieces. For each, place the interfaced pocket and pocket lining with right sides together and stitch round the side and lower edges, leaving a 1½in (4cm) gap in the lower edge through which to turn the pocket. Turn right side out, slipstitch gap in seam closed and press.

3 Place the completed front pocket on the bag front so it is 3¼in (8cm) up from the lower edge and 3¼in (8cm) in from the side edge on the left-hand side of the front piece. Stitch in place round the side and lower edges about ¼in (6mm) from pocket edge. If adding a back pocket, stitch this to centre of bag back, positioning upper pocket edge 3½in (9cm) from the top edge of bag.

Tip

As this is a big bag, using a firm craft-weight sew-in interfacing is key to achieving a professional finish. Sandwich a layer of wadding or quilted lining together with the fabric and interfacing for a firmer finish.

4 Pin bag front and back sections (with pockets now attached) to corresponding front/back interfacing sections. Baste together round entire outside edge, about ⅜in (1cm) from the raw edge. Make sure edges of exterior fabric align with edges of interfacing (see A).

5 Thread 7in (18cm) length of 1in (2.5cm) wide webbing tape through slot in one half of catch, double over so raw ends are even and pin together. Lay tape on interfaced bag front at point marked on front pattern template, at right-hand side of bag. Stitch tape (with catch attached) to bag front round both sides and top, about ⅛in (2mm) from the edge. Pin interfaced front/back pieces with right sides together. Stitch together at lower edge and press seam open flat. **Note:** Raw edges of tape will be encased in lower seam (see B).

6 Stitch front/back together at side and lower edges, leaving corners free. Fold lower corners of bag, matching centre of side seam with lower seam and pin in place. Stitch straight across to form a flat base for the bag. Each corner seam (and therefore the finished base of the bag) will measure about 2¾in (7cm) across (see C). Turn bag right side out and press.

7 Cover with a damp cloth and iron interfacing to wrong side of both flap pieces and pin flap sections with right sides together. Stitch together round sides and lower edges. Trim seam allowance to ¼in (6mm), clip into seam allowance at corners, turn flap right side out and press. Topstitch round flap about ⅜in (1cm) from the edge (see D).

8 Thread 14in (35cm) length of 1in (2.5cm) wide webbing through slot in other half of catch. Double over about 2¾in (7cm) to the back and pin in place. Lay tape on completed flap at line marked on pattern template (2in/5cm from the flap edge along right-hand side). Stitch to flap about ⅛in (3mm) from edge of tape down both sides and across bottom. **Note:** Folded edge of tape with catch will hang over flap at lower edge and raw end of tape will be at top (see E).

9 Mark centre of flap and bag back with pins. With centre points together, pin finished flap onto bag back, right outside of flap against right outside of bag back, with raw edges even. **Note:** Ensure webbing strip on bag front and flap align when flap is closed so both parts of fastener meet.

10 To make strap, cut 49in (125cm) length of the 2in (5cm) wide webbing and at one end thread it over centre bar of slider, folding over about 2in (5cm) to back. Tuck raw end under and stitch in place. Next thread on an O-ring, then thread raw end of webbing back through the slider buckle.

11 At other raw end, thread strap through another O-ring, fold over about 2in (5cm) to back, tuck raw end under and stitch in place. Take one 6in (15cm) piece of 2in (5cm) wide webbing and thread through O-ring at folded end. Double over and stitch raw ends together. Repeat at other end of strap with remaining 6in (15cm) length (see F).

12 On outside, positioned centered over side seams with handle facing downward, raw edges even and right side of handle against outside of bag, pin completed strap to bag and machine stitch in place (see G).

13 Place interior pocket with right side uppermost onto right side of back lining. **Note:** Upper edge of pocket should be about 2¾in (7cm) down from the top edge of back lining. Stitch in place around side and lower edges about ¼in (6mm) from edge. Stitch front/back lining pieces with right sides together at side and lower edges, leaving corners free. Leave a gap in the seam at the bottom of about 6in (15cm) for turning the bag through. Fold lower corners of bag matching seams and stitch straight across to form a base as you did for main bag (see H).

14 Insert bag into lining with right sides together, pin bag/lining together through all thicknesses round upper edges with raw edges even. Stitch about ⅜in (1cm) from edge. **Note:** You will be pinning through flap and strap too. Clip into seam allowance at intervals around the top.

15 Turn bag right side out through opening in bottom of lining and push lining to inside of bag. Turn flap upwards and roll lining with your fingers so it is not visible from the outside and pin in place all round top. Topstitch through all layers, about ⅝in (1.5cm) from top of bag. Insert plastic canvas or craft interfacing rectangle into bag bottom via gap in lining and push in place. Slipstitch gap closed, tuck lining back into bag and press.

16 On left underside of flap where shown on template, stitch rectangle of Velcro/riptape and stitch the hook part to top edge of front pocket so it aligns with piece on flap (see I). This will make the flap lie flat on both sides and will give extra security. To finish, stitch three buttons down the webbing strip at points marked with a cross on flap template (see J).

Knot Bags

These reversible Japanese knot bags are made with colourful fabrics in three useful sizes: hand, shoulder and cross-body. If you wish, you could topstitch around the openings or add beads or sequins for a more decorative look.

You will need:
- Pattern templates on pages 107–109
- Photocopier
- Cross-body bag: 43in (110cm) of fabric, 43in (110cm) of lining
- Shoulder bag 30in (75cm) of fabric, 30in (75cm) of lining
- Handbag 20in (50cm) of fabric, 20in (50cm) of lining
- Thread to match fabric
- Sewing machine
- Pins
- Fabric scissors
- Iron and ironing board

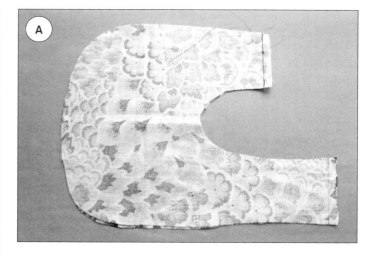

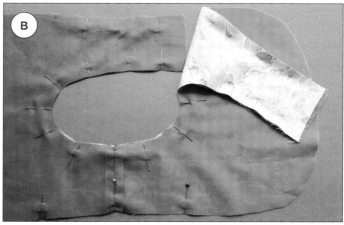

1 Using the templates, cut two in patterned fabric and two in lining fabric. Snip in ⅜in (1cm) at each side where marked on the pattern.

2 Taking the patterned pieces first, place them right sides together and join the smaller handle only, with a ⅜in (1cm) seam (see A). Press flat and sew the same seam on the lining pieces.

3 Place the patterned section on a flat surface with the patterned side facing upwards. Place the lining section on top, matching the raw edges, taking care to place the lining handle seam directly on top of the patterned handle seam. Pin and tack in place (see B).

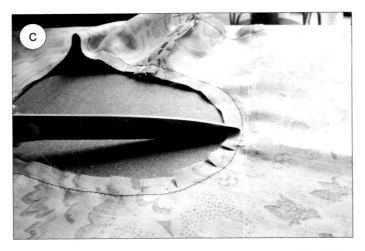

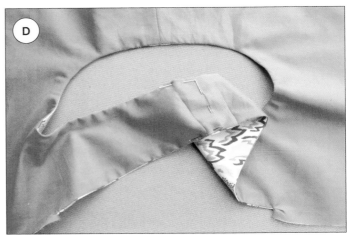

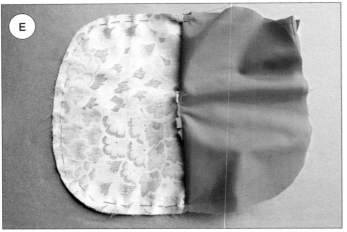

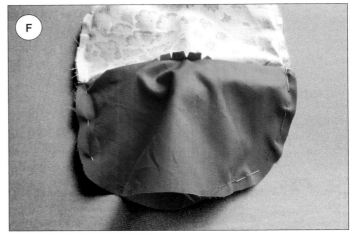

4 Starting at the outer edge of the smaller handle, machine a ⅜in (1cm) seam between each snip. At the outer edge of the long handle, start machining ¹³⁄₁₆in (2cm) down from the handle edge and machine to the snip. Machine the inner edge of the longer handles, stopping and starting ¹³⁄₁₆in (2cm) down from the long handle edge.

5 Snip into the curved edges at ⅝in (1.5cm) intervals to ensure a smooth curve when the bag is turned the right way round (see C).

6 Turn the bag the right way round by pulling the right side of the bag through the tunnel made by the small handle. Pull the longer handle sections through. Shake into place and using a steam iron press the bag flat.

7 Join the long handle with a ⅜in (1cm) seam by placing the patterned fabric right sides together. Press flat and then fold and pin the lining fabric neatly into place. Slipstitch by hand to finish off (see D).

8 To join the main body of the bag, place right sides together (pattern to pattern) pinning and then machining between each snip (see E).

9 Snip into the curved edges at ⅝in (1.5cm) intervals to ensure a smooth curve when the bag is turned the right way round.

10 Do the same with the lining but leave an opening along the bottom of about 2½in (10cm) (see F).

11 Turn the right way round and finally close the gap in the lining by folding the seam allowance to the inside, pressing and top-stitching in place, as close to the edge as possible.

12 Push the lining into the bag to finish. Fill with your things and push the long handle through the small handle to close.

> **Tip**
> Try changing the handles around to create different looks.

Stylish Shoppers

Shopping trips will be even more fun with these pretty, lightweight shopping bags. They're perfect to fold up and carry in your handbag, ready to use as soon you spot some irresistible bargains.

You will need:
- Pattern template on page 110
- Photocopier
- 40in (1m) patterned cotton fabric
- 40in (1m) polyester lining
- Thread to match fabric, plus contrasting thread
- Pins
- Large safety pin
- Sewing machine
- Iron and ironing board
- Fabric scissors

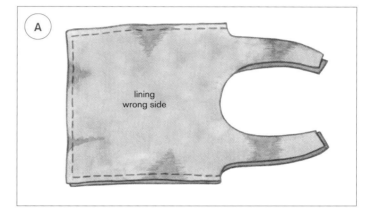

lining wrong side

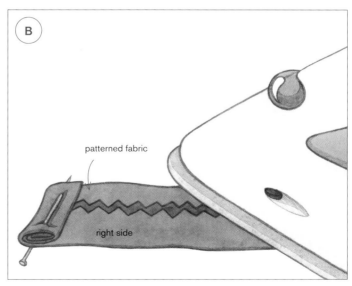

patterned fabric

right side

1 Place the pattern on the fold of the patterned cotton fabric and the polyester lining fabric and cut two of each. Put to one side.

2 Take the lining pieces, with right sides together sew a ⅝in (1.5cm) seam on all three sides, leaving the strap handles unsewn. Backstitch at either end (see A).

3 Now cut two pieces of the patterned fabric 8½in x 2½in (22 x 6cm) for the cord channel. Fold one in half lengthways, press with the iron. Open up and bring in the longer edges into the centre crease, press again. With the shorter ends, fold in ⅜in (1cm), press and then fold again ⅜in (1cm) in (see B), press and sew to hold in place. Repeat to create a second cord channel.

4 To attach the cord channels to the main bag, take one of the channel pieces and position on the right side of the patterned bag, 5½in (14cm) in from the right-hand corner on a diagonal and pin in place (see C). Repeat process with the other patterned fabric bag piece but 5½in (14cm) in from the left-hand corner.

5 Sew the channels on to the fabric using a running stitch along the longest edges, leaving the short ends open. Use a backstitch at either end for strength. Neaten off the threads.

6 Now with right sides together, repeat Step 2 with the patterned bag. Turn right side out and press.

7 Put the main bag inside the lining bag so that you have right sides together and pin. Then sew a ⅝in (1.5cm) seam around the handles but stop stitching 4in (10cm) from the top of the straps. Backstitch to secure.

8 Carefully turn the bag right side out through one of the handles (it will be difficult at first). Pull out the other handle.

Tip
When sewing with polyester lining, make sure you use the correct-sized sharp needle to prevent puckering.

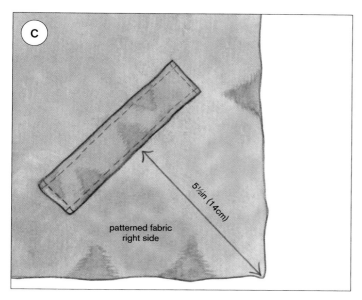

patterned fabric
right side

5½in (14cm)

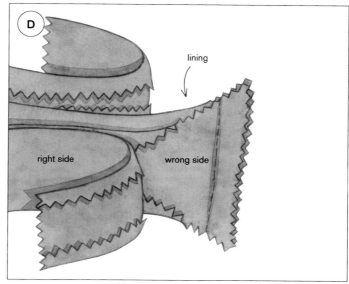

lining

right side

wrong side

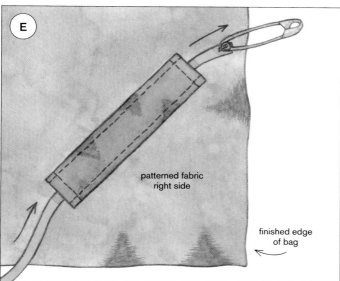

patterned fabric
right side

finished edge
of bag

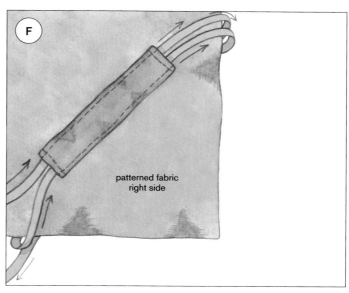

patterned fabric
right side

9 Now sew the straps of each set together, making sure you have sewn each strap to the strap beside it, not the one in front of it (see D). Press the seams open and then press the seam allowance on the straps. Match the strap lining seams to the main bag and pin.

10 Press all edges of the bag and topstitch all using a contrasting thread to make a crisp clean edge.

11 For the sash that will be the drawstring part of the bag, cut a 40 x 1³⁄₁₆in (100 x 3cm) piece of the patterned fabric, fold and press with the iron as in Step 3, then sew a running stitch along all the open edges. Neaten off threads.

12 Take a large safety pin and attach to one end of the sash you have just made. Start threading the sash through the top end of the right-hand corner channel (see E), bring through and up on the reverse channel, then again through the top of the right corner channel until it comes back through to join the other end (see F). Tie together and hide knot in the channel.

Tip
To create a contrasting corner pocket, cut a
7½ x 7½in (19 x 19cm) square, fold in half on the diagonal,
press and sew into position on the corner. Do this
to both sides then place the sash channel
above each corner.

Duffel Bag

This sturdy drawstring bag in bright candy stripes is ideal for packing a picnic, towel, sunscreen and swimsuit in for a day of fun at the beach. The deckchair fabric is hardwearing and will stand up to plenty of use from all the family.

You will need:

- 40in (1m) striped deckchair fabric
- 20in (50cm) cord fabric in a coordinating colour
- 40in (1m) plain cotton fabric, for the lining
- 60in (1.5m) No.6 cotton piping cord
- Thread to match fabric
- 20in (50cm) medium-weight iron-on interfacing
- One packet of 11mm brass eyelets
- Small hammer
- Tailor's chalk
- Set square
- Sewing machine
- Iron, ironing board and handkerchief or pressing cloth
- Pins
- Fabric scissors

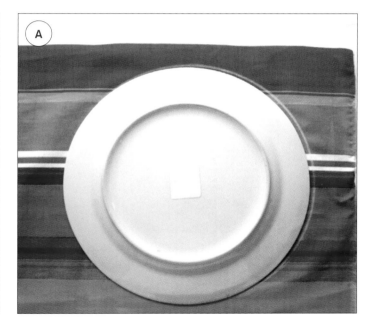

1 For the main body of the bag, on the reverse side of the striped fabric draw a rectangle approximately 34 x 18in (87 x 45cm). For the base, draw around a dinner plate measuring approximately 10½in (27cm) across (see A). Cut out and use these pieces as templates to cut the same shapes from the lining fabric.

2 Cut one further circle from iron-on interfacing. Cover with a damp handkerchief or pressing cloth and iron the interfacing onto the back of the striped base.

3 Cut a small pocket shape for your phone from the lining fabric: this one measured 5½ x 4¾in (14 x 12cm).

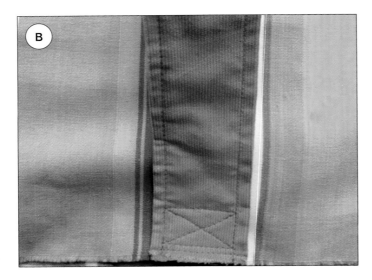

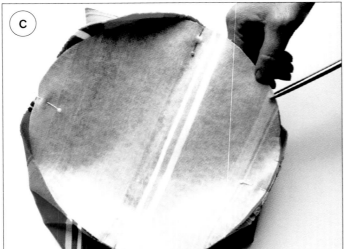

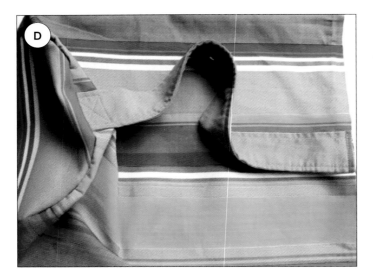

4 For the handle, take the cord fabric and on the reverse side draw a rectangle measuring 19¼ x 4¾in (49 x 12cm).

5 For the eyelet band, also in the cord fabric, draw a rectangle measuring approximately 34 x 4¾in (87 x 12cm). Cut the same shape from interfacing and iron onto the back of the cord fabric.

6 To begin making the bag, start with the handle and fold it in half lengthways with the right side on the inside and sew a ⅜in (1cm) seam down the long edge. Turn the right way round, press lightly with an iron and topstitch ³/₁₆in (5mm) from either edge.

7 For the main body of the bag, take the striped fabric and fold it in half with the right side facing inwards. Sew a ⅜in (1cm) seam down the side and press it open. Turn the right way round.

8 Now to attach the handle. At the bottom of the bag, centre one edge of the handle to sit over the side seam, sew in place with a ⅜in (1cm) seam. To make the joint stronger, sew a rectangle and then a cross inside it (see B). Join the handle at the top of the bag by machining a ³/₁₆in (5mm) seam.

9 Mark the bottom edge of the bag into quarters. Turn inside out.

10 Mark the edge of the base into quarters. Pin the base to the bag, matching the four quarter marks. Then snip in ³/₁₆in (5mm) at intervals around the edge of the base, as this will help it to fit the body of the bag better (see C).

11 Stretch the base into place, pin and machine a ⅜in (1cm) hem around the edge. Turn the right way round (see D).

12 To make the eyelet band, firstly fold in half widthways with the right side outwards and press with an iron along the folded edge. Then open it flat and fold in half lengthways and sew a ⅜in (1cm) side seam along the two short ends. Press the seam open. Fold the band back into shape with the right sides showing.

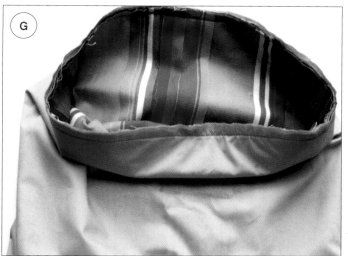

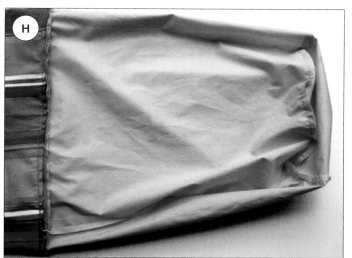

13 Position the eyelet band around the outside upper edge of the bag with the raw edges aligned. Pin and machine a ⅜in (1cm) seam. Press and then topstitch at either edge of the band (see E).

14 Mark the centre for each eyelet with a cross. Here the bag was folded in half and measured in 1³⁄₁₆in (3cm) from the centre front. The other eyelets were spaced at 4¾in (12cm) intervals. This process was then repeated around the other side of the bag.

15 Working on a solid surface, place the cutting tool over the cross and give it a firm tap with the hammer. Place the eyelets in the holes, add the backs and use the tool and hammer to secure in place.

16 To make the lining, firstly add the pocket for your phone. Measure 4in (10cm) down from the top edge at the centre of the lining piece and topstitch in place (see F).

17 The side seam of the lining needs to have a gap for turning the bag out. The gap is sewn up once the bag is finished. Sew down 6in (15cm) from the top and sew up 2in (5cm) from the bottom; this will leave a 10in (25cm) gap.

18 To add the lining, place the lining over the bag with right sides together and raw edges matching along the top of the bag. The eyelet band will be sandwiched between the outer fabric and lining. Machine a ⅜in (1cm) seam (see G).

19 Add the lining base in the same way as the outer base (see H). Pull the whole bag through the gap in the lining and machine the gap closed.

20 Push the lining into the bag and thread the cotton piping cord through the eyelet holes, knot either end, pull and tie in a bow to close the bag.

Festival Bag

Keep your essential belongings in this laid-back boho bag. It's the perfect
accessory for a fun weekend with your friends. Just add some braids
and flowers to your hair and you've nailed festival chic.

You will need:
- Pattern templates on page 111
- Photocopier
- 80in (2m) patterned fabric (here we have used 40in/1m
  each of two different patterns)
- 40in (1m) oilcloth, for the lining
- 20in (50cm) iron-on interfacing
- 47in (1.2m) of 1in (2.5cm) cotton webbing
- One 1in (2.5cm) metal slider
- Two 1in (2.5cm) metal loops
- Toggle
- 60in (1.5m) thin piping cord
- 60in (1.5m) elastic
- Safety pin
- Tailor's chalk
- Fabric marker
- Ruler
- Thread to match fabric
- Fabric scissors
- Pins
- Handkerchief or pressing cloth
- Sewing machine
- Iron and ironing board

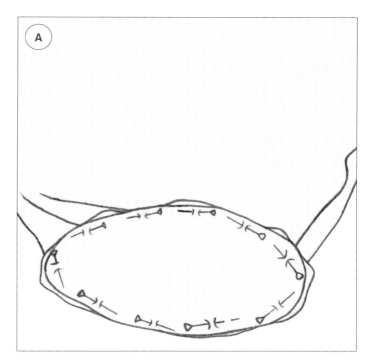

1 Cut out all pattern pieces. All seam allowances are ⅜in (1cm).
Begin by making up the oilcloth lining. Place the two main bag
pieces on top of each other with right sides facing and machine
a ⅜in (1cm) seam down both sides. Use a fabric marker to mark
the bottom edge of both pieces into halves. Take the oval base
and mark it into quarters with fabric marker on the reverse.

2 With right sides together, pin the base to the bag (see A),
lining up the side seams and halfway markers with the four
points marked on the base. Stretch the base into place as you
go and sew a ⅜in (1cm) seam around the edge. Put to one side.

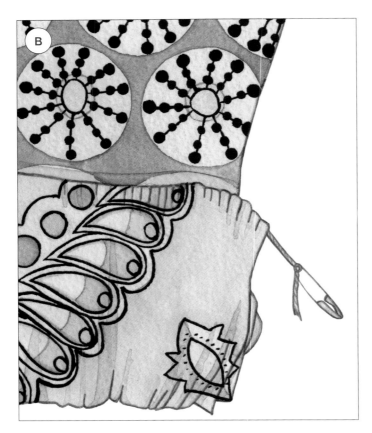

3 Take the fabric pieces of the main bag. Cover with a damp cloth and iron on 2½in (6cm) strips of interfacing along the top on the reverse side. Mark the position of the finished pockets with tailor's chalk on the outside of the bag, using the paper pattern as a guide.

4 To make the elasticated pockets, take a pocket piece and make a casing along one long edge by folding over ⅜in (1cm) and folding again and topstitching along the free edge. Using the paper pattern and tailor's chalk, mark in the lines where the pocket will be stitched to the bag.

5 Use a small safety pin to thread the elastic through the casing – use more elastic than you need so that it sticks out at either edge when lying flat (B). Measure in 2in (5cm) from one edge only and machine over the casing to fix the elastic in place.

6 Using the longest machine stitch, sew a gathering thread along the bottom of the pocket. Place the pocket over the front of the bag. Pull the gathering thread until the pocket is the same size as the bag. Pin in place.

7 Pull the elastic until the pocket top fits the bag. Measure in 2in (5cm) from the other edge of the casing and machine the elastic in place (the 2in/5cm gap stops the shape of the bag from distorting once it is sewn together).

8 Machine the pocket in place by stitching down the two chalk lines and by sewing down the sides. Repeat the process on the other side of the bag.

9 Join the bag at the side seams by placing one section on top of the other with right sides together. Use a fabric marker to mark the bottom edge of both pieces into halves.

10 Take the oval fabric base and iron on the interfacing. Mark into quarters. With right sides together, pin the base to the bag and sew in place, lining up the side seams and halfway markers with the four points marked on the base.

11 Drop the lining into the bag with wrong sides together. Pin and stay stitch by machine along the top edge to hold them together.

12 Now to attach parts of the handle. Take 3¼in (8cm) of webbing and thread it through a metal loop. Fold the webbing in half and position in the outside centre of the bag, raw edges level with the top of the bag. Machine in place. Repeat on the other side (see C).

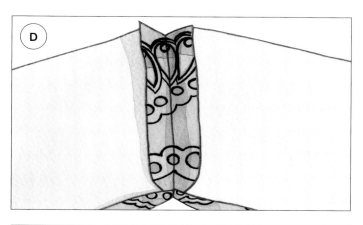

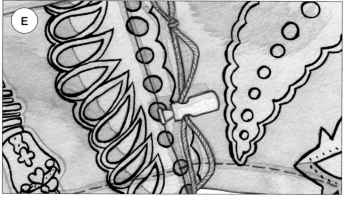

13 To make the gathered top opening of the bag, take the two top section pieces and join at one side, press seam open. Make a ⅜in (1cm) casing along the shorter edge, folding the edges in to neaten them and leaving a gap for threading the cord. Join the other side seam (see D).

14 Place the top on the outside of the bag with right sides together and raw edges matching. Pin and machine in place. Push into the bag. Press and topstitch through all layers ⅜in (1cm) in from the edge.

15 Now to finish the handle. Cut a 40in (1m) piece of webbing and thread through the centre of the slider. Topstitch in place.

16 Thread the other edge of the webbing from front to back through one of the metal loops. Thread it through the edge of the slider and from front to back through the other loop. Fold up and machine in place.

17 Finally, use a small safety pin to thread the narrow cord through the casing on the top of the bag. Attach a toggle and tie the ends (see E).

Slouch Bag

The epitome of minimalist, relaxed style, this linen slouch bag with knotted shoulder strap and contrast piping will lend a modern, utilitarian edge to any outfit.

You will need:

- Pattern template on page 112
- Photocopier
- 40in (1m) taupe-plain linen
- 47¼in (1.2m) piping cord
- Fabric scissors
- 20in (50cm) mustard cotton fabric for piping
- Thread to match fabric
- Sewing machine and zipper foot
- Pins and needle
- Iron and ironing board

1 Use the template to cut out the bag pattern. Cut out all pieces. Begin with the base of the bag. Join the two bottom pieces by placing right sides together. Pin in place and machine a ⅜in (1cm) seam. Overlock the edges and press the seam open.

2 For the top section of the bag, place centre front right sides together, matching the raw edges, and machine a ⅜in (1cm) seam. Overlock the edges and press open. Repeat for the other side of the bag.

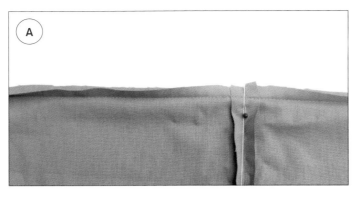

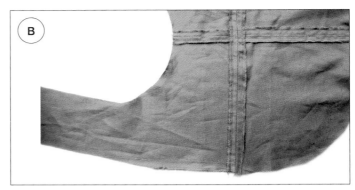

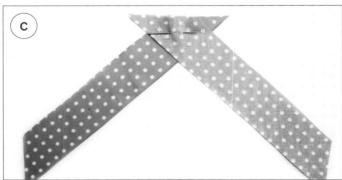

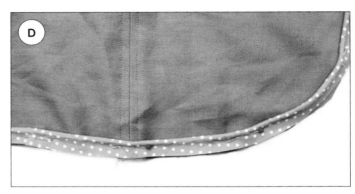

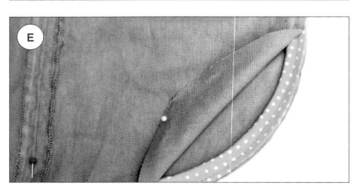

3 Join the top to the base by placing right sides together and matching raw edges. Push a pin through the centre of the seams and keep in place while machining the top and base together (see A). Overlock edges and press open (see B). Overlock the inner edges of the handles.

4 To make the piping, cut 1³⁄₁₆in (3cm) wide bias strips and join until you have enough to cover the length of piping cord. To make bias strips, fold the fabric in half diagonally. Press along the fold and use it as a guide to mark the 1³⁄₁₆in (3cm) parallel lines. To join the strips, cut the ends at an angle along the straight grain and with right sides together pin two strips with right sides facing and seam (see C). Press the seams open. Fold the bias strip over the cord and tack by hand or machine quite close to the cord.

5 Place one half of the bag on a flat surface facing upwards. With raw edges matching, pin the piping around the edge of the bag. Tack in place (see D).

6 Place the other section on top, sandwiching the piping in place. Add a zipper foot to your machine. Pin, tack and machine through all layers with a ⁹⁄₁₆in (1.5cm) seam. Overlock all layers together (see E).

7 To finish the inner edge, press over a ³⁄₈in (1cm) seam to the inside and topstitch in place. The top corners will need to be trimmed and folded inwards as you stitch. Finally, tie a double knot at the top of the handles (see F).

Tip
Use the same pattern pieces to add a contrasting lining.

Gabardine Backpack

Smart and practical, this gabardine backpack will be eternally fashionable, and is the perfect accessory for cycling about town. Team it with skinny jeans and ballet pumps for a classic Parisian-chic look.

You will need:
- Pattern template on page 113
- Photocopier
- 40in (1m) cotton gabardine fabric
- 20in (50cm) patterned fabric for the lining
- 157½in x 1in (4m x 2.5cm) black cotton webbing
- 51 x 1³⁄₁₆in (1.3m x 2cm) black bias binding
- One pair of leather straps with buckles
- Two 1in (2.5cm) rectangular metal rings
- Thread to match fabric
- Pliers (optional)
- Pins and needle
- Air-erasable pen
- Sewing machine
- Iron and ironing board
- Fabric scissors

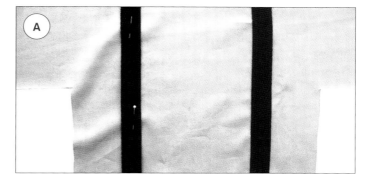

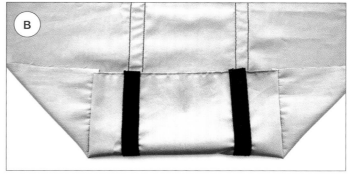

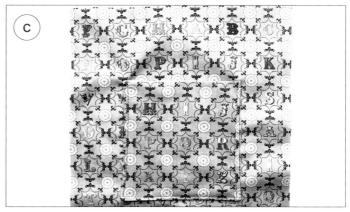

1 Photocopy the pattern templates and cut out all of the pieces. Use an air-erasable pen to mark the position of the cotton webbing on the right side of the bag. Pin and machine the webbing in place by sewing close to the outer edges (see A).

2 To join the front corners, place right sides together and sew a ⅜in (1cm) seam, stopping ⅜in (1cm) in from the outer end. Press the seam open (see B). Machine the front lining corners in the same way.

3 To make the pocket for your phone, place the squares on top of each other with right sides together. Machine around the edges, leaving a gap of 2in (5cm) for turning through. Turn the right way, press, pin and machine in place to the back lining (see C).

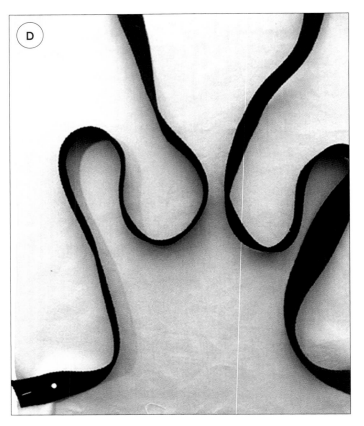

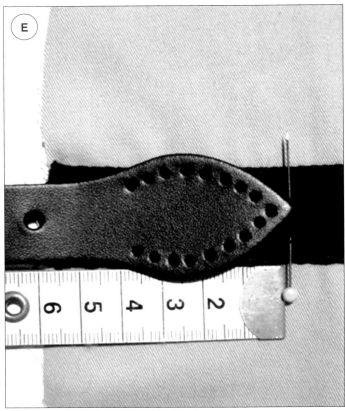

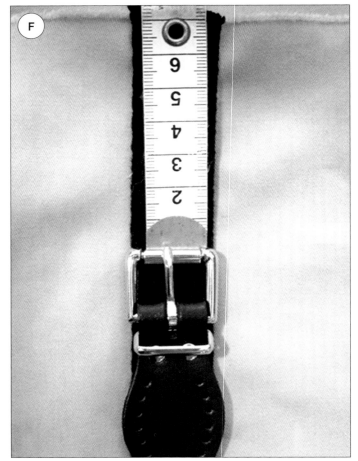

4 To join the back and front lining sections together, with right sides together line up the raw edges and place the front to the back. Pin and machine in place.

5 Add two 27½in (70cm) webbing straps to the back section where marked on the pattern. Machine firmly within the seam allowance (see D).

6 Now to add the buckles. The top buckle is positioned with the leather point of the buckle 2½in (6cm) from the raw edge (see E) and the bottom buckle is 2¾in (7cm) from the top of the metal end of the buckle to the raw edge (see F). The buckles are sewn on by hand. You may find a pair of pliers useful for pulling the needle through the holes.

7 Attach the back of the bag to the front in the same way as the lining. With wrong sides facing, drop the lining into the bag and line up the top raw edges. Pin and tack together.

Tip
Change the size of the pocket to fit your phone.

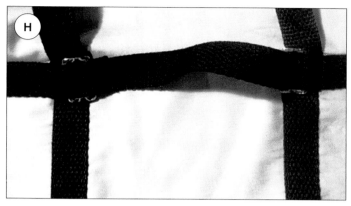

8 To finish the front and side edges, open one edge of the bias binding and place the binding on the inside of the bag. Pin and machine in place, folding the outer ends in. Fold the binding over to the front of the bag, pin in place and machine along the folded edge.

9 Now to make up the small handle. Take a piece of cotton webbing measuring 11in (28cm). Push each end through a rectangular ring, fold the ends over by ⅜in (1cm) and machine in place (see G).

10 Cut two pieces of webbing 4¾in (12cm) long and attach to the other ends of the rectangular rings.

11 Pin the handle to the top of the bag ⅜in (1cm) in from the back edge and machine in place.

12 Place the lining to the top of the bag with wrong sides facing, lining up the raw edges. Tack around the edges and apply the bias binding in the same way as before.

13 Join the top to the bag, place right sides together, lining up the webbing stripes (see H). Pull the lower bag lining out of the way and machine in place. Fold the edge of the lining over and slipstitch in place. Finally, machine a small pleat in the binding, 1³⁄₁₆in (3cm) deep at the top of each side of the bag.

Pretty Tote

Taking inspiration from original designs from the eighteenth and early twentieth centuries, a collection of striking V&A fabrics makes for a beautifully elegant and unique tote bag.

You will need:

- Pattern templates on pages 114–115
- Photocopier
- Two fat quarters* of main fabric
- One fat quarter of secondary fabric
- Two fat quarters of lining fabric
- 29½in (75cm) very heavy calico (or heavy fabric stiffener)
- Pair of 18in (46cm) leather piped handles
- Strong thread to match your handles
- ¾in (18mm) diameter magnetic snap
- Thread to match fabric
- Sewing machine
- Fabric scissors
- Needles and pins
- Iron and ironing board

*A fat quarter measures approximately 20 x 22in (50 x 57cm)

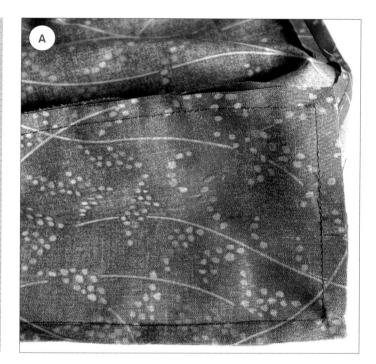

1 Cut out all your fabric pieces using the templates.

2 With right sides facing, join the two lining pieces (pattern piece A) along their bottom edge with a ⅜in (1cm) seam. Press the seam open with a hot iron.

3 With right sides facing, align the centre of the base of one lining gusset strip (pattern piece B) with one end of the base seam of the main lining piece. Pin or tack away from this point in both directions, to ⅜in (1cm) before each corner of the gusset piece. Machine stitch from the centre base point along your pin or tack line with a ⅜in (1cm) seam. When you reach the point ⅜in (1cm) from the corner, and with the machine's needle down (anchoring the layers of fabric), raise the machine's foot and twist the two layers of fabric so that you will turn a corner on the gusset while continuing straight along the main piece. Lower the machine foot and continue feeding the fabric through to stitch a ⅜in (1cm) seam along the remainder of the side edges (see A). Repeat this along the other side of the gusset.

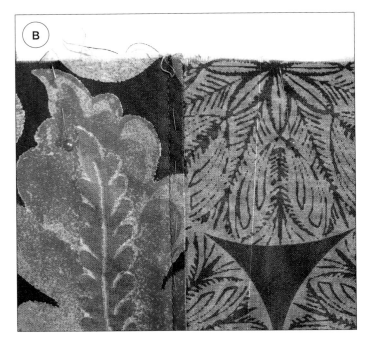

4 Repeat Step 3 with the second gusset on the other side of your lining.

5 With right sides facing, pin or tack the long bottom edge of one outer top piece (pattern piece C) to one long edge of an outer bottom piece (pattern piece D). Stitch a ⅜in (1cm) seam. Do the same with the other main and base pieces. Iron the seam towards the bottom with a hot iron.

6 Join the bottom edges of these two pieces by laying them on top of each other right sides together, pinning or tacking and sewing a ⅜in (1cm) seam by machine. Use a hot iron to press this seam open.

7 Lay these joined pieces right side up on the strip of heavy calico and pin around all edges. Stitch a line of tacking 4in (10cm) from either end to denote the top edge fold of your bag. Pin or tack through all layers, just below the main piece and base piece joins, on the front and back. Topstitch through all layers ³⁄₁₆in (4mm) below the seam (see B). Trim the calico all around, following the edge of the patterned fabric.

8 Make both outer gusset panels: with right sides facing, pin or tack the short bottom edge of one top outer gusset piece (pattern piece E) to the short edge of one bottom outer gusset piece (pattern piece F). Stitch a ⅜in (1cm) seam. Do the same with the other gusset pieces. Iron the seam to the base piece side with a hot iron. Back the two gusset strips with heavy calico and topstitch as in Steps 5 and 6.

9 Now join the outer gussets to the outer main piece by following the instructions in Steps 3 and 4, while aligning the change of fabric seams of the main and bottom fabrics as accurately as you can and manipulating the fabrics again to follow the angles at the fold line of the top edge.

10 Fix the two parts of the magnetic snap in the positions indicated on the pattern, following the manufacturer's instructions (see C).

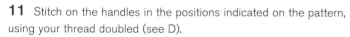

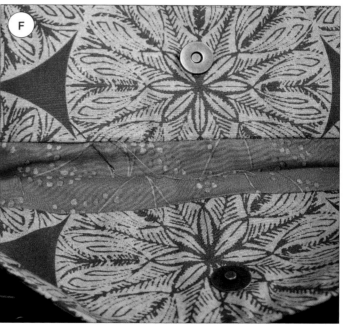

11 Stitch on the handles in the positions indicated on the pattern, using your thread doubled (see D).

12 With the outer of the bag wrong way out and the lining right way out, slip the lining into the outer bag and pin and tack the top raw edges of both together (see E).

13 Sew a ⅜in (1cm) seam around the top edge, leaving an 8in (20cm) gap at one side, starting and finishing with reverse stitching to strengthen the sides of the gap. Press the seam towards the main fabric and away from the lining.

14 Turn the bag out through the gap and fold the top edge of the outer down on the inside of the bag along your tacked line from Step 7. Close the turning out gap with small stitches by hand (see F).

15 Working from the inside, pin or tack through all layers ⅜in (1cm) below the fold of the top edge and topstitch by machine.

Patchwork Holdall

Raid your remnants box and use up scraps of shirting stripes to make this spacious patchwork holdall. Sturdy and stylish, it makes a great carry bag for your shopping or the ideal beach bag.

You will need:

- Scraps of striped fabrics for the patchwork tiles
- 20in (50cm) natural linen for outer base
- 47¼in (1.2m) floral fabric for lining
- 47¼in (1.2m) heavy fabric stiffener
- 118 x 1³⁄₁₆in (3m x 3cm) wide strong tape
- Sewing machine
- Thread to match fabric
- Pins and a needle
- Ruler or measuring tape
- Card
- Iron and ironing board
- Fabric scissors
- Rotary blade and cutting mat (optional)

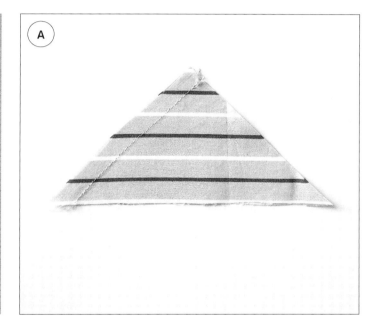

A

1 Draw three right-angled triangles: (measurements of longest edges) large 6¾in (16.5cm), medium 4⅓in (11cm), small 2¼in (5.5cm) plus ⅜in (1cm) seam allowance all round each piece. Cut them out of card.

2 Use your templates to cut your fabric pieces: ensure your stripes are always running in the direction of the longest side of the triangular templates; this will generally leave the two shorter sides cut on the bias. Cut four pieces of fabric for each tile square. You will need 4 large tiles, 12 medium tiles and 16 small tiles.

3 Piece your tiles together: place two triangles right sides together and stitch a ⅜in (1cm) seam along one short edge. Try to make all the stripes align, but don't worry if they are a bit uneven; you are working on the bias and the fabrics will potentially stretch and loose their shape slightly, but any quirkiness will add character to your unique patchwork (see A). Stitch the corresponding pair of triangles in the same way. Press both seams open with a hot iron.

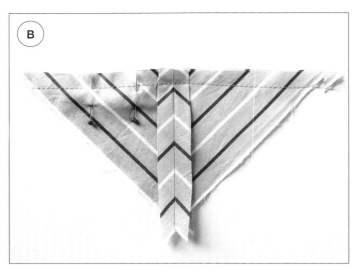

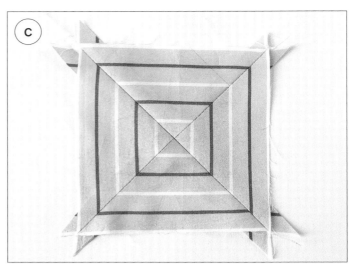

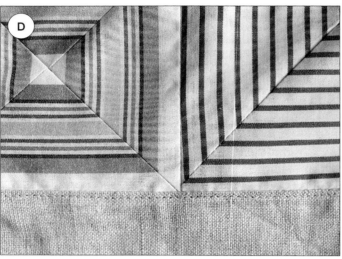

4 With right sides facing, stitch a ⅜in (1cm) seam along the long edge, trying to keep the two seams from Step 3 aligned (see B). Press the seam open with an iron (see C).

5 Follow Steps 1 to 4 to make all your tiles.

6 Following the diagram on page 115, take your time to lay out the tiles to make two panels until you are happy with the colour balance and pattern distribution of the fabrics. Join all pairs of small tiles with a ⅜in (1cm) seam and with right sides together. Press the seam open with a hot iron. Join the tiles to form the five vertical strips of the chart, pressing the seams open. Finally, join all the strips, pressing the seams open.

7 Cut two pieces of linen measuring 22½ x 7½in (57 x 19cm). Join the bottom edge of each patchwork panel to one long edge of a piece of linen with a ⅜in (1cm) seam and right sides facing. Press the seam towards the linen side with a hot iron. Topstitch along the plain linen side of this seam (see D).

8 Cut two lining pieces measuring 22½ x 8½in (57 x 47cm) each. Cut your stiffener in half so that it measures 20in (50cm) wide and 23⅝in (60cm) long and lay it down. Lay the patchwork and linen outer piece on top, right side up. Now lay the lining on top so that all their top edges align. Pin or tack along the top edge and machine stitch a ⅜in (1cm) seam. With a hot iron, press the lining up over the raw edges of the seam. Now fold the lining fabric over the raw edges to the back of the panel, so that it binds the top of the panel by ⅜in (1cm). Press with a hot iron. Tack or pin along the top edge and topstitch (see E). Stay stitch by machine around the three raw sides of both the front panel, the stiffener (now sandwiched between the outer and inner pieces) and the lining. Trim any excess stiffener with scissors. Repeat Step 8 with the second panel.

9 Cut your heavy tape into two 59in (150cm) lengths to form the handles. Position one end so that it aligns with the bottom edge of the panel on the linen, 3½in (9cm) from the centre. Pin or tack in place through all layers to the top bound edge of the fabric piece. Do the same with the other end, making sure the tape is not twisted at the top where it forms a handle. Stitch by machine ⅛in (3mm) in from either edge of the tape, starting at the bottom edge, turning at the top edge of the panel, stitching along the width of the handle and then back down to the bottom edge of the panel (see F). Do the same with the other end of the handle. Repeat with the second fabric panel.

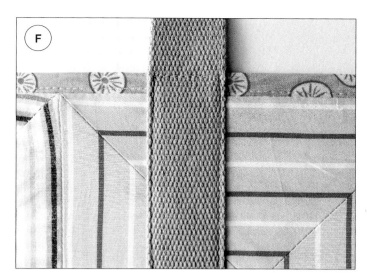

10 Place the two panels together, wrong sides facing. Machine stitch a ⅜in (1cm) seam around the side and bottom edges. Trim the raw edges to 3/16in (5mm) and turn the bag wrong sides out. Press the seams with a hot iron and pin or tack before stitching a ⅜in (1cm) seam all around (creating a French seam), reverse stitching at the beginning and end to give it extra strength. You can also zigzag stitch a few times back and forth across either end of this seam to close it if looks messy.

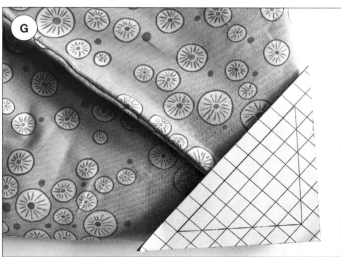

11 Using an iron, press the seam at the base of your sack to one side. Place the medium-sized triangle template on the corner and mark its long edge with tacking stitches or pins (see G). Cut two 4¾ x 1 9/16in (12 x 4cm) pieces of linen. Fold one long edge of each piece in by ⅜in (1cm) and press with an iron. Take one piece and, opening it out, place the pressed fold face down on one of your drawn corner lines so that the majority of its width lies towards the centre of the bag and it extends approx. ¾in (2cm) at either end. Pin or tack in position, then machine stitch a seam along the pressed line through all layers.

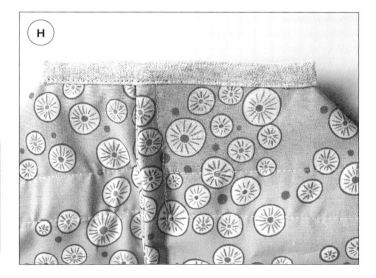

12 Cut off the triangular corner tip to align with the ⅜in (1cm) seam edge created by the strip of linen. Fold the ends in and then fold the strip of fabric over twice to form a hem encasing all the raw edges. Pin or tack and stitch down either by hand or machine (see H). Turn your bag right side out.

Tip
For extra strength, stitch back and forth a few times across the width of the handles where they meet the top of the panels.

Travel Bag

Every traveller should have stylish luggage. Why not make yourself this fantastic oversized bag that's perfect for all your travel essentials? A bold print in bright colours will ensure it stands out in the crowd.

You will need:
- Pattern templates on pages 116–117
- Photocopier
- 49¼in (1.25m) main fabric
- 10in (25cm) plain fabric
- 197in (5.25m) contrasting bias binding
- 197in (5.25m) piping cord
- 59in (1.5m) lining fabric
- 20in (50cm) iron-on interfacing
- 78¾in (2.5m) heavyweight fusible stabilizer
- 29in (74cm) metal or heavy weight plastic zipper
- Thread to match the main fabric, the piping cord and the lining fabric
- Fabric scissors
- Sewing needle and pins
- Sewing machine
- Zipper foot
- Iron and ironing board
- Handkerchief or pressing cloth
- 'D' ring (optional)
- Stitch unpicker

1 Cut your fabric, lining, interfacing and fusible stabilizer as follows:

A side: cut two in main fabric

B side 'scuff bottom': cut two in plain fabric

C side: cut two in fusible stabilizer and two in lining fabric

D zip panel: (place on fold and) cut two in main fabric, cut two in lining fabric, cut two in iron-on interfacing

E end pockets: cut two in main fabric, cut two in lining, cut two in iron-on interfacing

F base: cut one in plain fabric, cut one in lining fabric, cut one in fusible stabilizer

You don't need pattern pieces for the handles, just cut your fabric as follows:

G handle: cut two strips 13 x 50cm in main fabric

H handle stiffening: cut two strips 1³⁄₁₆ x 20in (3 x 50cm) in fusible stabilizer.

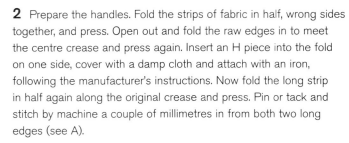

2 Prepare the handles. Fold the strips of fabric in half, wrong sides together, and press. Open out and fold the raw edges in to meet the centre crease and press again. Insert an H piece into the fold on one side, cover with a damp cloth and attach with an iron, following the manufacturer's instructions. Now fold the long strip in half again along the original crease and press. Pin or tack and stitch by machine a couple of millimetres in from both two long edges (see A).

3 Prepare the covered piping. Place the cord down the centre of the opened out binding. Fold the fabric back down to encase the cord and stitch it in place by machine using a zipper foot and with thread to match the binding.

4 Prepare the bag sides. Cut a 21in (53cm) length of covered piping cord and lay it along the top edge of the right side of one B piece of plain fabric so that the raw edges of both the fabric and the piping align. Pin or tack and sew by machine as close to the piping as you can, using the zipper foot. Now lay one A piece of main fabric right sides together so that its bottom edge aligns with the top piping at the edge of the B piece (see B). Align the raw edges, pin or tack, and sew by machine close to the piping. With a hot iron, press the seam towards the plain fabric.

5 Repeat Step 3 to make the second side of your bag.

6 Attach both C pieces of fusible stabilizer to the wrong side of the completed side pieces using an iron and following the manufacturer's instructions.

7 Starting and ending at the centre of the bottom of each side piece, pin or tack covered piping all the way around the edge, taking care to create smooth curves at the corners, overlapping the two raw ends by approx. 1½in (4cm) and curving them away and over the edge of the side pieces (see C).

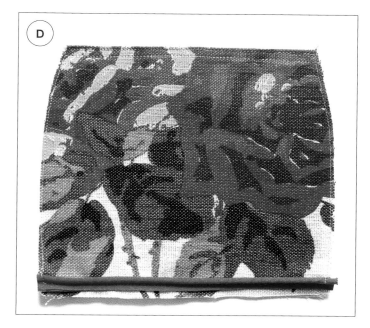

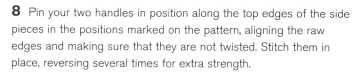

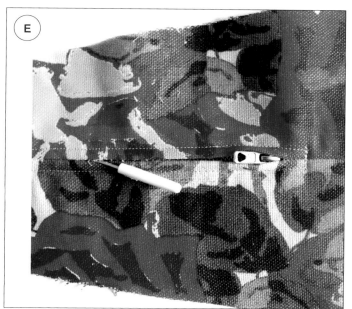

8 Pin your two handles in position along the top edges of the side pieces in the positions marked on the pattern, aligning the raw edges and making sure that they are not twisted. Stitch them in place, reversing several times for extra strength.

9 Prepare the pockets. Iron the interfacing E pieces on to the wrong side of the main fabric E pieces. Place a main fabric E piece face down onto a lining E piece and pin or tack along the top straight edge. Sew a ⅝in (1.5cm) seam by machine. Turn right side out, press and topstitch along the seam edge. Stitch 8¾in (22cm) of piping along the bottom raw edge (see D).

10 Prepare the zip panel. Attach a double thickness of D piece iron-on interfacing onto the wrong side of each of the two D pieces of main fabric. Place the two pieces right sides together. Align the long straight edges and pin or tack. Sew a ⅝in (1.5cm) seam from the left-hand edge to the 'end of zip' point on the pattern, reverse stitching at the beginning and end for strength. Do the same at the right-hand side.

11 Now change your machine to a long basting stitch and sew along the centre section to complete the seam.

12 Press the seam open with a hot iron. With the wrong side up, lay your zip right side down along the pressed seam. Pin or tack it in place. Turn the panel right side up and, using the zipper foot, stitch approx. ³⁄₁₆–⁵⁄₁₆in (5–7mm) from the seam all around the zip through all layers, reverse stitching back and forth several times at either end of the zip for extra strength.

13 Use a stitch unpicker to cut the basting stitches along the centre of the panel to reveal the zip from Step 11 (see E).

14 Lay one pocket right side up on one end of the zipper panel (also right side up), aligning the bottom edges. Pin or tack all the way around (see F). Stay stitch along the three raw sides of the pocket ⅛in (3mm) in from the edges. Repeat with the other pocket pieces.

15 Finally, attach the F piece of fusible stabilizer to the wrong side of the F piece of plain fabric. Lay one short end to align with the bottom of the pocket, right sides together. Pin or tack and stitch as close to the piping as you can.

16 Repeat Step 15 with the other end of the base and the opposite pocket.

17 Attach the side pieces to the zipper/pocket/base strip. Pin one side of your zipper/pocket/base strip to the outside edge of one of your side pieces, right sides facing. Take your time to do this, easing and teasing the straight edge of the zipper/pocket/base strip to sit comfortably on the curves of the corners of the side piece (see G). Stitch all the way round as close to the piping as possible – this is quite difficult as the layers of fabric are quite thick, so take it slowly. Turn right side out and check how close against the piping you've managed to sew your seam. If there are areas you think you can improve on, don't unpick them, but stitch across the area again, machining slowly as you go.

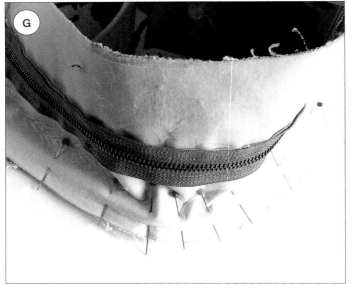

18 Prepare the lining. Place the two D pieces of lining together. Align the long straight edges and pin or tack. Sew a ⅝in (1.5cm) seam from the left-hand edge to a point 6¾in (17cm) in, reverse stitching at the beginning and end for strength. Do the same at the right-hand side. Press the seams open and then remove the tacking. Lay one short end of lining piece F, to align with one end of the lining zipper panel, right sides together. Pin or tack and stitch a ⅜in (1cm) seam. Repeat at the other end of the base piece.

19 Sew the lining side panels to the lining zipper and bottom panel, just as you did for the outer bag.

20 With the wrong side out, put the lining inside the bag. Pin or tack the lining to the inside of the zip and attach with small slipstitches by hand (see H).

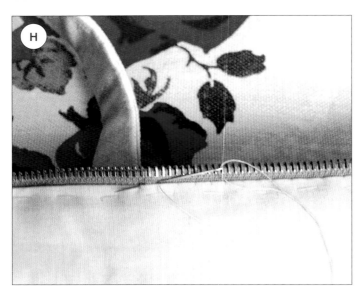

Tip
Here, a 'D' ring for keys has been inserted under the piping at the centre top of one panel at Step 6. Make a tab for it in exactly the same way as you made the handles, but omit the fusible stabilizer.

Market Basket

It's so easy to imagine yourself strolling around the local market stalls of a pretty French village with this beautifully stylish, yet sturdy, ticking-fabric shopping basket on your arm.

You will need

- 40in (1m) cotton ticking
- 60in (1.5m) heavyweight fusible fabric stiffener
- 40in (1m) cotton wadding
- 40in (1m) lining fabric
- Sewing machine
- Thread to match fabric
- Fabric scissors
- Needle and pins
- Strong white cotton yarn, cord or string
- Large wool needle
- 55 x 6in (1.4m x 15cm) leather or herringbone tape
- 60 x ⅜in (1.5m x 1cm) diameter jute rope
- Ruler
- Bradawl
- Iron and ironing board
- Handkerchief or pressing cloth
- Bulldog clips

1 Cut the fabrics for the sides of the basket: one rectangle in each of the outer fabric, the inner fabric, the wadding and the stiffener to measure 48 x 19¾in (122 x 50cm) (cut the ticking so that the stripes run vertically across the shorter measurement of the rectangle).

2 Cover with a damp cloth and use an iron to fuse the stiffener to the lining fabric. Lay the stiffened fabric over so that it is lining side down. Lay the wadding over it and finally the ticking on top, right side up. Pin all the way around. **Note:** Do not use tacking – as you quilt the stripes you may well have to re-pin to avoid tucks and wrinkles.

3 Stitch vertical lines by machine following the stripes of the fabric – here the lines were roughly ¾in (2cm) apart, but yours may differ depending on the scale of the stripe in your fabric. This may be difficult to manoeuvre under your machine foot and you may find it easier to work from the outside to the centre from the top down, then turn your work around and work from the other edge to the centre to meet your previous two lines of stitching. The 'sandwich' of fabrics will be fairly stiff; here the stitching was started on the right-hand edge and the strip was rolled up on the right as it was worked across, securing the top and bottom ends of the roll with bulldog clips.

4 Trim the 'sandwich' of stiffened and quilted fabrics to measure 15¾ x 44in (40 x 112cm) and zigzag stitch around all four sides to minimize fraying.

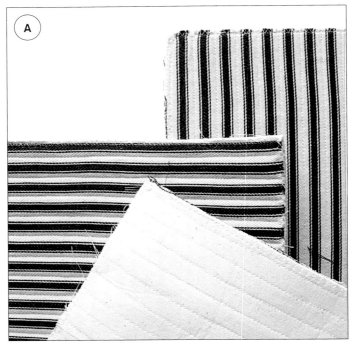

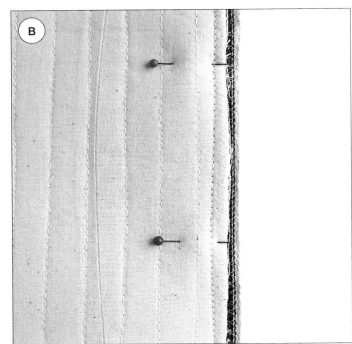

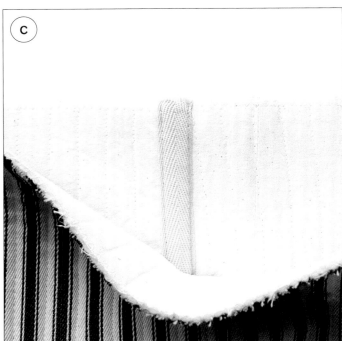

5 Cut the fabrics for the base of the basket: two pieces of ticking, one of stiffener and one of cotton wadding to measure 17¼ x 13¼in (44 x 34cm).

6 Repeat Steps 2 and 3, replacing the lining fabric layer with the second piece of ticking (see A). Trim to 13¼ x 9½in (34 x 24cm), cutting curves at the corners before zigzag stitching around the raw edges.

7 Fold the large rectangle in half, right sides together, so that the short ends meet. Position so that one edge extends ³⁄₁₆in (5mm) beyond the other, pin and stitch a ³⁄₈in (1cm) seam (see B).

8 Press the seam to one side and cover it with the herringbone tape. Sew along the length of the tape ⅛in (2mm) in from either side to cover the raw edge of the side seam (see C).

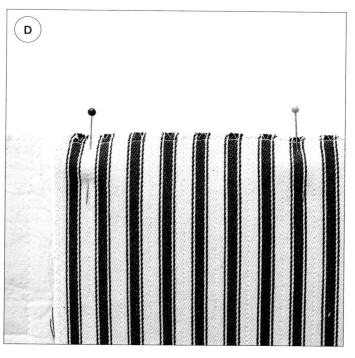

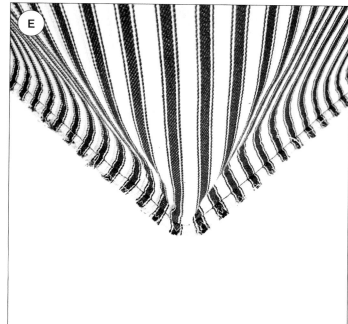

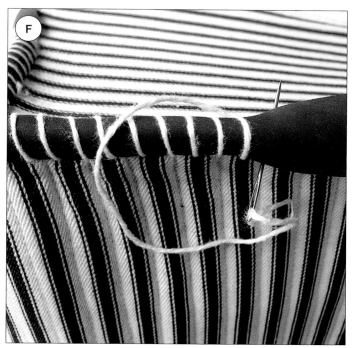

9 Turn the basket sides right side out. Pin the base piece to the bottom edge of the side piece, wrong sides facing (see D). Take your time to do this, easing and teasing the straight edge of the sides to sit comfortably around the curves of the base piece. Pin and stitch all the way round ⅜in (1cm) from the edge – this will be quite difficult as the layers of fabric are quite thick, so take it slowly (see E).

10 Cut two strips of leather 2 x 55in (5 x 140cm) and use white string or cotton and a large wool needle and overstitch to bind the four sides of the base. In doing so you will cover the raw edges of the fabric. You will not be stitching through the leather, but just beyond the edge of it (see F). Following the stripes in the sides of the bag will help you to make fairly even stitches. To finish, tie the two ends of string together and tuck behind the leather.

11 Repeat Step 10 to bind the top edge of your bag.

12 To make the handles, cut two lengths of rope 14in (35cm) long and two lengths of leather 27¾ x 2in (70 x 5cm).

13 Use a bradawl to pierce a hole ⅜in (1cm) apart, ³⁄₁₆in (5mm) in from the edges along both long edges of the leather strips, starting 4in (10cm) from either end.

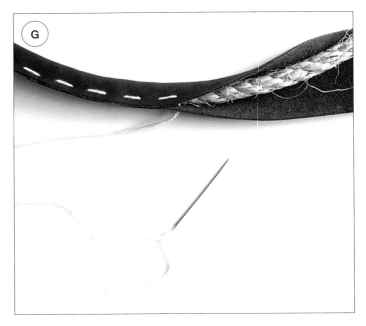

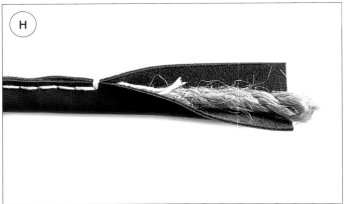

14 Lay a length of rope along the length of the wrong side of one strip of leather. Using string and a wool needle, sew the two long edges of the leather together, wrong sides facing: start at one end using running stitch (see G). When you reach the other end make two overstitches (perpendicular to your running stitch line to hold the two sides together securely) and then work your way back to the beginning in running stitch, filling the gaps. Finally, finish with another two overstitches, tie the thread ends together, trim to ⅝in (1.5cm) and tuck into the leather seam to hide them (see H).

15 Trim the rope in each handle so that it measures ¾in (2cm) short of the leather at each end. Round off all the corners of the leather with sharp scissors and use the bradawl to punch 17 holes ⅜in (1cm) apart around both ends of each handle. Sew the handles centred on either side of the basket 5⅛in (13cm) apart – starting at one end using running stitch. When you reach the other end, make two overstitches (perpendicular to your running stitch line to hold the two sides together securely) and then work your way back to the beginning in running stitch, filling the gaps. Finally, finish with another two overstitches, tie the thread ends together, trim to ⅝in (1.5cm) and tuck into the leather seam to hide them (see I).

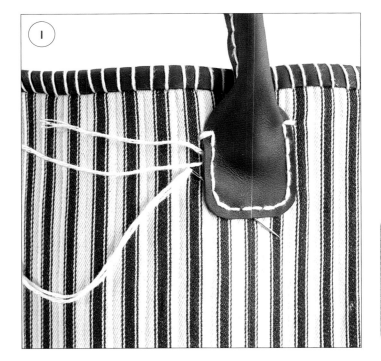

Tip
You can use strong herringbone tape rather than leather for the edge binding and handles. Fold up either end of the handles to avoid fraying.

Felted Bag

This colourful felted bag is a fun way to carry your knitting, yarn and needles around with you when you're out and about. Snap fasteners make it easy to open and close, and the leather handles are comfortable and strong to hold.

You will need

- Six balls Thick 'n' Thin Rowan yarn in your base colours (three dolomite blue, three basalt green)
- Four balls Thick 'n' Thin Rowan yarn in contrasting colours 1 (two pyrite red, two shale purple)
- Two balls Thick 'n' Thin Rowan yarn in contrasting colour 2 (pumice yellow)
- Two pieces of linen for lining 21½ x 12½in (55 x 32cm)
- Two strips of heavyweight fusible stiffener 21½ x 1¾in (55 x 4.5cm)
- 41 x 1½in (104cm x 4cm) wide herringbone tape
- Two 28in (71cm) leather bag handles
- Three magnetic snap fasteners
- 15¾ x 5½in (40 x 14cm) bag bottom (see tips, page 76)
- Four bag feet
- Needle and pins
- Sewing machine
- Thread to match fabric
- Fabric scissors
- Iron and ironing board
- Handkerchief and pressing cloth

1 Take one ball of your base colour (blue) and rewind it into two balls. These will be used for A and G in the chart on page 117.

2 Cast on 118 sts.
Follow the chart as follows:
A half ball base colour (blue)
B one ball contrast colour 1 (red)
C one ball base colour (blue)
D one ball contrast colour 2 (yellow)
E one ball base colour (blue)
F one ball contrast colour 1 (red)
G half ball base colour (blue)

Work in stocking stitch, using separate balls for each 'sawtooth' stripe of colour and twist the yarns around each other as you change colours. Keep knitting until the first of the three contrast colour balls of yarn run out. Continue to work one row in the base colour then cast off in the base colour.

3 Repeat Steps 1 and 2, this time using green as your base colour, purple as contrast colour 1 and yellow as contrast colour 2 again. You now have two pieces of knitting ready for felting.

Tip

Felting your hard work can be a bit frightening – you can always wash it more than once but at a slightly lower temperature in order to have more control. Alternatively, use a heavy wool, heavy felt, or felt an old (100% wool) blanket. Your yarn must be 100% wool to felt successfully.

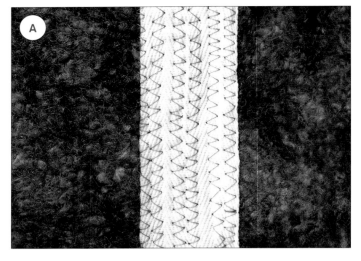

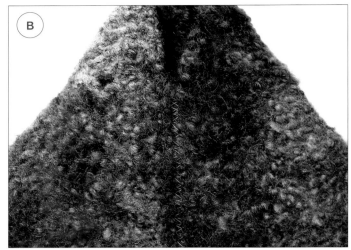

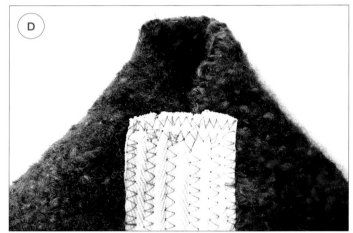

4 Felt your knitting by washing the two pieces at 140°F (60°C). You can wash it in a zipped netting washing bag. You can also put an old pair of jeans into the machine with your knitting: the friction against the jeans during washing will accelerate the felting progress.

5 Give them a good tug in all directions and pin the knitting out to dry out fully on a large cushion or an ironing board to help control the shape. You should end up with two pieces of thick woollen felt, each measuring more than 22 x 13½in (56 x 34cm). Cut the two pieces down to 21¼ x 12½in (54 x 32cm) with sharp scissors.

6 Butt the two pieces of felt together along one long edge, right sides up. Set your machine to a wide zigzag stitch and join the two pieces by slowly feeding them and pushing them snugly together under the machine foot as you work.

7 Turn the felt over. Pin or tack a 19in (48cm) length of herringbone tape centred over the join of the two pieces. Zigzag stitch along the length of the herringbone tape six times – this is the wrong side of your work (see A).

8 Turn the felt right side up and, with the joined seam vertically in front of you, fold the top left and right-hand corners down to meet the central seam. Zigzag along the two edges to join them, just as you did in Step 1, to make one of the side seams. You will not need to stitch right into the corner (which would also be very difficult!) because you will be cutting this off in Step 12 to create a box corner (see B).

9 Tack a 11in (28cm) length of herringbone tape along the side seam join. Zigzag stitch up and down over the tape just as you did in Step 8 (see C).

10 Repeat Steps 7 and 8 on the other side to complete the second side seam.

11 With the bag still inside out, match the side seam with the bottom seam to create a point at the corner. Pin to hold them together. It is very important that you match the seams exactly; this will make your finished corner look good (see D).

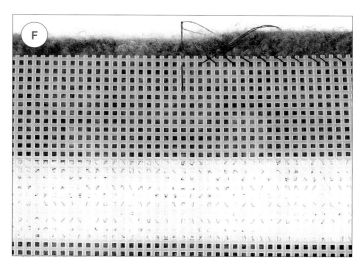

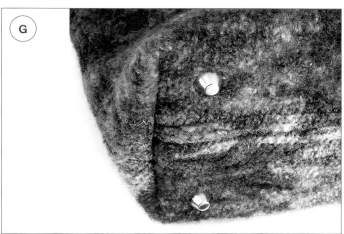

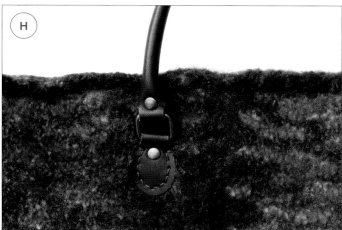

12 Mark the line of the box corner measured 4¾in (12cm) from side to side, and 2⅜in (6cm), measured from the tip of the corner. Sew across the point twice, reverse stitching at the beginning and end for extra strength. Trim away the peak to ³⁄₁₆–⅜in (5mm–1cm) from the line of stitching (see E).

13 Cut your bag base to size and baste onto the bottom of your bag between the two box corner seams and centred over the base (herringbone) seam (see F).

14 Turn your bag right side out. Fix the bag feet in position 1⅛in (3cm) in from each corner, fixing them through the bag base for extra strength (see G).

15 Stitch the handles on to your bag – 5⅛in (13cm) from the side seams and 3in (7.5cm) from the top edge (see H).

16 Take one lining piece and lay it out horizontally in front of you. Fold the top edge down 2in (5cm) and press. Open it out again. Take one strip of heavyweight fabric stiffener and place it adhesive side down on the lining below and butting up to the fold crease. Cover with a damp cloth and iron on. Repeat with the second lining piece (see I).

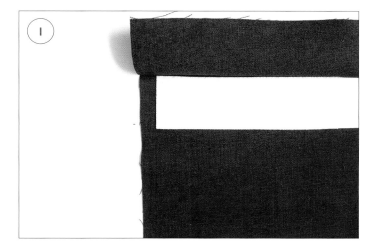

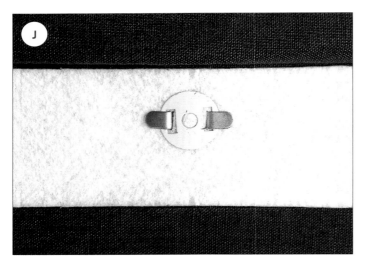

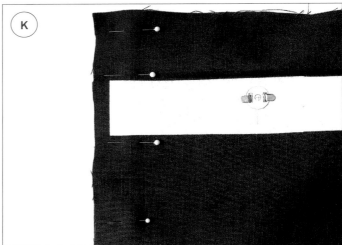

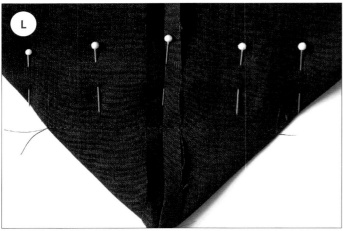

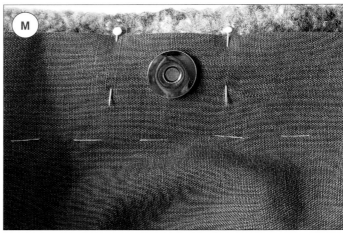

17 Fix the three magnetic snaps to the two lining pieces: one centrally and the other two 6in (15cm) to either side of this one and ⁹⁄₁₆in (1.5cm) from the top edge of the stiffener (see J).

18 Place the two lining pieces together with the magnetic snaps 'snapped' together. Pin or tack the side and bottom edges and stitch with ⅜in (1cm) seams (see K).

19 Press the seams open and follow the instructions in Steps 11 and 12 to make two box corners (see L).

20 Fold the top edge down along the crease, tack down and stitch 1½in (4cm) from the top edge. Place inside the felt bag, tack in position ⁹⁄₁₆in (1.5cm) from the top of the felt, and machine stitch ⅛in (3mm) from the top of the lining all the way around (see M).

Tips

Here, a 13½ x 7½in (34 x 19cm) bag bottom has been used. Once cut to the right width, the offcuts were used to extend the length at one end by overlapping it by approx. 1½in (4cm) and stitching it together.

Measure your knitting once felted and while still wet – at this point you can stretch it if it is a bit small.

Follow the manufacturer's instructions for stitching on the handles, magnetic snap fasteners and bag feet.

Reversible Shopper

Tactile bamboo handles make this pretty shopping bag a statement piece. Choose patterned fabrics to complement your summer clothes, and make two bags in one that can simply be turned inside out if you fancy a change.

You will need

- Pattern templates on page 118
- Photocopier
- 23½in (60cm) each of 44in (112cm) wide main and contrast fabric
- Medium-weight fabrics: cotton, linen
- 60in (1.5m) of 35½in (90cm) wide medium-weight iron-on woven interfacing (when cutting this out, make sure the grain line on the pattern follows the grain of the woven interfacing)
- Thread to match fabric
- One pair of 7in (18cm) diameter round bag handles
- Fabric scissors
- Pins
- Tailor's chalk
- Sewing machine
- Iron and ironing board
- Handkerchief or pressing cloths

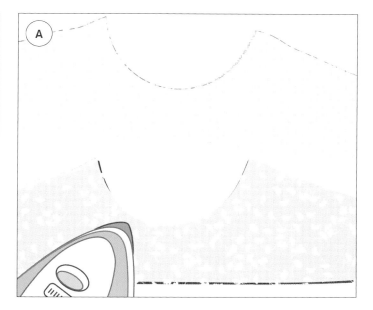

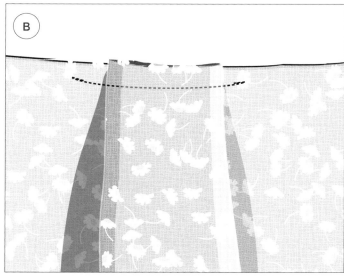

1 Place the interlining, with the coated side down, on the wrong side of the fabric. Cover with a damp cloth and press to fuse pieces (see A). Allow to cool before stitching.

2 Make the pleats at the top of the bag pieces by folding along the solid lines, with right sides together, matching the broken lines. Lay the pleats towards the centre front. Stitch along the seam line to hold the pleats in place (see B).

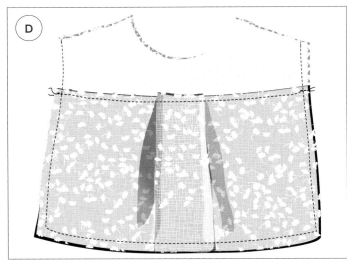

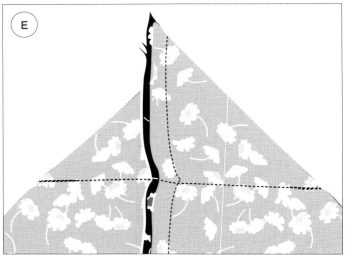

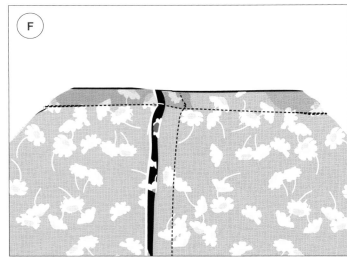

3 With right sides together, matching the notches, pin and stitch a contrasting yoke to the pleated edge of each of the bag pieces.

4 Trim the seams and press them towards the yoke. Topstitch the lower edge of the yoke (see C).

5 With right sides of two pieces together, matching the notches, stitch the side and lower edges along the 9/16in (1.5cm) seam (see D). Trim the seams. Join the remaining pieces in the same way to make two identical bags.

6 With wrong sides together, align the side and lower seams at a corner so they meet, forming a point. Press well. Mark out a line, using pins or tailor's chalk, 2¾in (7cm) from the point and sew a straight seam following the line (see E). Trim the seam to ⅜in (1cm) (see F). Repeat for the other corners to create a flat base on both of the bags.

7 Staystitch the 9/16in (1.5cm) seam along the top edges of each yoke. Trim to 3/16in (5mm) from the seam line. Turn under and press along the staystitching (see G).

8 With right sides together, slip one bag inside the other, matching the seams. Stitch the top-side edges, pivoting the needle at the side seams and leaving the yokes open. Trim the seams and snip into the inverted corner at the side seams, taking care not to cut into the stitching (see H). Turn the bag right side out, pushing one inside the other, and press well.

9 Cut a 3½in x 21¼in (9 x 54cm) strip of fabric to make the loops to hold the handles. With right sides together, stitch along the long edge, allowing a 9/16in (1.5cm) seam. Turn right side out and press.

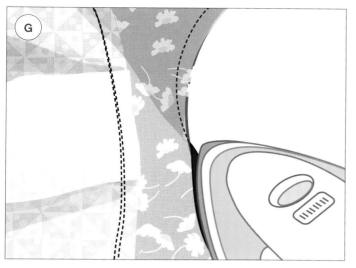

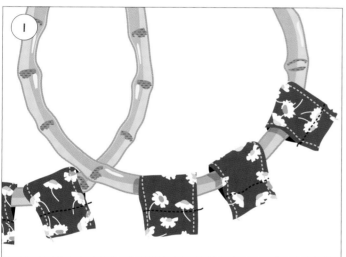

10 Cut the strip into six 3½in (9cm) lengths. Topstitch down each long edge.

11 Wrap three loops around each handle and sew along the 9/16in (1.5cm) seam (see I).

12 Slip the three loops attached to one handle inside the pressed edges of the yoke on one side of the bag, matching the seam allowances. Position the central loop at the centre front and the remaining loops ⅜in (1cm) from the corner on each side. Pin in place, matching the pressed edges of the yokes and inserting extra pins to keep the edges together. Pin the remaining handle and yoke in the same way on the other side of the bag (see J).

13 Topstitch all around the top edges of the bag, stitching through all layers to attach the loops holding the handles.

Tips

Pick out a bright colour from the detail in the printed fabric for the topstitching to make it stand out.

A different colour thread can be used on the bobbin, but don't mix the fibres as this can lead to problems when sewing.

Embellished Bag

Delicate lace, ribbon and beads are used to make the pretty floral decorations that embellish this vintage-inspired little evening bag. It's made in sumptuous velvet and lined with a vintage scarf.

You will need

- Pattern template on page 117
- Photocopier
- 11¾ x 23⅝in (30 x 60cm) main fabric
- A pretty vintage scarf to line the bag
- 11¾ x 23⅝in (30 x 60cm) sew-in fleece interfacing
- Thread to match fabric
- Stranded embroidery thread
- 6in (15cm) sew-in purse frame
- 47¼in (120cm) purse chain
- Fabric scissors
- Needle and pins
- Tailor's chalk
- Sewing machine
- Fabric glue (optional)

To embellish the bag
- Remnants of fabric, felt, lace, ribbon, beads, bead headpins
- Round-nose pliers

1 Place the main fabric pieces with right sides together and sandwich them between the fleece. Place the lining pieces with right sides together. Pin and stitch the lower edges of both the lining and main fabric pieces between the dots, along the ⅜in (1cm) seam (see A). Trim and notch the curves.

2 With right sides together, slip the lining inside the main fabric bag. Working on one side at a time, sew the top edges together between the dots. Leave an opening of around 3⅛in (8cm) on one side to turn. Trim and notch the curves (see B).

3 Turn the bag right side out. Turn under the raw edges of the opening and sew together by hand or machine (see C).

4 Work on one side of the bag at a time to attach the frame. Mark the centre of each side of the bag opening with tailor's chalk. Using three strands of embroidery thread, knot the end and fasten to the centre of one side of the bag opening. Pass the needle, from the inside of the frame, through the central hole to the front. Pull up tight on the thread and then tuck the top of the bag into the frame. The pointed end of a small pair of scissors can be used to poke the edges into the channel, but take care not to tear the fabric.

5 Working from the centre to the hinge, neatly stitch one side of the opening of the bag to the frame. After stitching through the final hole by the hinge, work back towards the middle by sewing between the previous stitches (see D). Keep checking the bag is right inside the frame. Fasten off on the inside of the bag where it won't be seen. Repeat for the other side of the opening to attach the first side of the bag. Attach the other side of the bag to the frame in the same way.

6 Pick out floral and paisley patterns from pieces of lace and cut them out (see E).

7 Cut a 1½ x 23⅝in (4 x 60cm) strip of fabric. Here, satin fabric has been used and strips were cut from the leftover pieces of the vintage scarf that lined the bag. Adjust the length and width to make a larger or smaller rosette. Fold the fabric in half lengthways and tie a knot in the end. This will be the centre of the rose and the foundation to start forming the petals around. Wrap the folded fabric around the knot, stitching it down at the base to hold it in place. Twist and fold the fabric to form the petals, stitching the fabric to the base at the same time to secure. Fold the end of the strip of fabric under, and stitch it to the base to finish the rosette (see F).

8 Make felt flowers by cutting five individual petals from felt. Sew them together and stitch beads in the centre (see G).

9 Thread beads onto the headpins and use round-nose pliers to curl the end of the pin into an eye.

10 To make the honeysuckle flower, cut a 1¾in (4.5cm) diameter semicircle. Prepare three beaded headpins (see Step 9) for each flower and stitch them together in the centre of the long, straight edge of the semicircle. Fold the felt in half so the straight edges meet, encasing the beaded wires. Sew together the straight edges to form a cone shape. Cut five petal shapes and stitch them to the top of the cone. To make the stems, add a few beads to doubled thread secured to the top of each honeysuckle before stitching the flower to the bag, so they hang freely (see H).

11 Turn under the raw ends of the ribbon and fold the length into loops. Stitch the top of the loops together to hold them in place (see I).

12 Lay the lace on the front of the bag and arrange the flowers over it, tucking the ends of the beads and ribbons under the floral decoration. Pull the lining out through the opening of the bag to prevent catching it in the stitches when sewing the decorations on. Stitch everything neatly and securely in place (see J). Finally, attach the chain to the frame of the bag.

Tips

Before cutting the fabric out, check for tiny holes in the scarf by holding it up to a window.

The rosettes can be made using lengths of ribbon instead of strips of fabric. The ribbon won't need to be folded, but choose the width you would like your finished rosette to be.

The fabric can be glued to the frame to hold it in position, making it easier to stitch in place. Working on one side at a time, apply fabric glue to the channel of the purse frame. Insert the top of the fabric bag and allow the glue to dry. Attach the other side of the frame in the same way and allow to dry before stitching.

Reversible Tote

This elegant reversible tote bag in complementary linens has a handy detachable purse. Smart and capacious, it's ideal for slinging over your shoulder when you head to the shops.

You will need

For the tote bag

- 17¾ x 35½in (45 x 90cm) linen for outer
- 17¾ x 35½in (45 x 90cm) linen for lining
- 11¾ x 8¾in (30 x 22cm) linen for pocket
- 4 x 2in (10 x 5cm) linen for D-ring tab
- ¾in (2cm) D-ring
- 63in (160cm) of 1⅛in (3cm) wide webbing

For the purse

- 5½ x 9¾in (14 x 25cm) linen for outer
- 5½ x 9¾in (14 x 25cm) linen for lining
- 12½ x 1⅛in (32 x 3cm) linen for tab
- 4in (10cm) zip
- One swivel trigger clip

- Sewing machine
- Piping/zipper foot
- Needle and pins
- Threads to match fabrics
- Fabric scissors
- Iron and ironing board
- Pencil or tailor's chalk
- Knitting needle

TOTE BAG

1 Make the tab with the 4 x 2in (10 x 5cm) piece of linen: fold the strip in half along its apex and press. Open the fabric out again and fold each long edge in to meet the central crease then fold again. Pin or tack and stitch along each long edge.

2 Feed the D-ring onto the tab, align the two raw ends and zigzag stitch them together.

3 Fold your outer fabric in half, right sides together (now 17¾ x 17¾in [45 x 45cm]), and press. Pin or tack the two side seams (the fold making the bottom of your bag) and stitch ⅜in (1cm) seams by machine. Press the two seams open.

4 Put your hand inside your work and push one corner so that the bottom corner of the side seam forms a point and the pressed seam aligns with the fold/crease of the bottom of the bag. Mark 3½in (9cm) from each side of the point and join them with a line in pencil or tailor's chalk (see A).

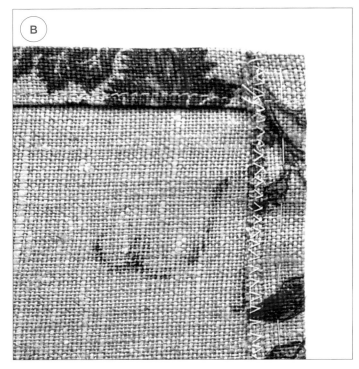

5 Pin or tack and machine stitch along this line to make a box corner. Trim the excess/point to ⅜in (1cm) from the stitch line.

6 Repeat Steps 2 and 3 with the other bottom corner.

7 Take your pocket piece, and with the wrong side facing you, fold one long edge over ⅜in (1cm) and ⅜in (1cm) again. Pin or tack and stitch the hem by machine. Zigzag along the three raw edges before turning them in ⅜in (1cm). Press with a hot iron and tack in place (see B).

8 Take the lining piece and lay it down right side up and vertically in front of you. Position and pin or tack the pocket (right side up and hemmed edge furthest away from you) 4¾in (12cm) from the raw top edge and centred on the fabric. Stitch around the two sides and bottom edges, reversing or stitching a triangle at the beginning and end for extra strength (see C).

9 Repeat Steps 1 to 4 with the lining, but this time insert the tab in one side seam, 2¾in (7cm) from the top edge and stitching across it several times for strength when you stitch the side seam (see D). On the other seam, leave 6in (15cm) of the seam unsewn to turn your bag through later.

10 Turn your lining piece right side out and insert it into the outer (still inside out). Align the raw edges of the outer and the lining and pin all the way around.

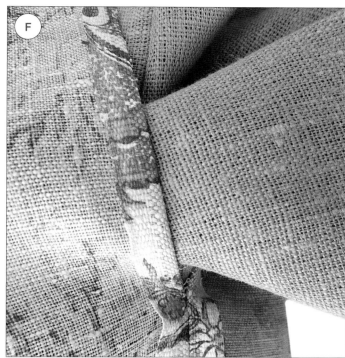

11 Cut the webbing in half to make the handles and, being careful to ensure they're not twisted, pin them between the two layers 5½in (14cm) from each side seam, protruding 1½in (4cm) beyond the raw edges of the two layers of fabric (see E).

12 Stitch a ⅜in (1cm) hem around the top edge, reverse stitching a couple of times over the ends of both handles. Turn your bag right side out through the turning gap (see F).

13 Close the turning gap in your lining with hand stitching (see G).

14 Press the top edge with a hot iron and topstitch along it. Sew another line of stitching 1⅜in (3.5cm) below the top edge, catching the ends of the handles between the two layers of fabric as you do so (see H).

PURSE

1 Make the long, thin purse tab with the 12½in x 1⅛in (32 x 3cm) piece of linen: fold the strip in half along its apex and press. Open the fabric out again and fold each long edge in to meet the central crease then fold again. Pin or tack and stitch along the edge to hold in place.

2 Feed the swivel trigger onto the tab, align the two raw ends and zigzag stitch them together.

3 Lay the outer fabric down, right side up and vertically in front of you. Lay the zip face down, aligning with the top edge. Lay the lining fabric right side down on top, again with the top edge aligning. Pin or tack all three layers together (see I).

4 Stitch the zip in by machine, sewing as close to the zip teeth as you can using a piping foot. Fold down the two layers of fabric on either side of the zip and press. Topstitch close to the zip – this will prevent the lining from catching in the zip in future (see J).

5 With the outside fabric facing you and the zip furthest away, fold up the bottom edge to align with the top edge of the zip and pin in place. Turn your work over, fold up the bottom edge of the lining and align its raw edge with the top of the zip. Pin or tack all three layers together (see K).

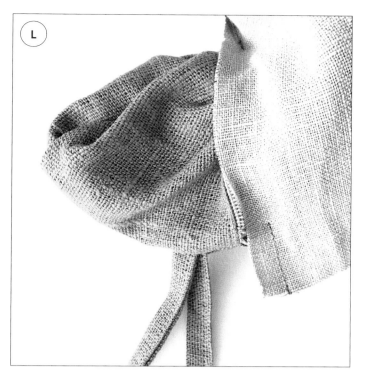

L

M

6 Now repeat Step 2. With your work still inside out, manipulate the fabrics so that the fold in the lining is nearest you, the zip in the middle, and the fold in the outer fabric furthest away. Pin or tack down the two sides of the lining, marking a 2⅜in (6cm) turning gap on one side. Pin or tack one side of the outer fabric. On the other side, insert the long purse tab and swivel trigger between the two layers of linen, leaving its two raw ends protruding just ⁹⁄₁₆in (1.5cm) from the zip. Pin and tack. Stitch ⅜in (1cm) seams down both sides of your work, across the zip ends. Remember to leave the turning gap unstitched and sew several times back and forth across the protruding tab ends to give them extra strength.

7 Turn the purse right side out through the turning gap (see L).

8 Close the turning gap with small stitches by hand.

9 Prod the bottom corners gently with the end of a knitting needle to make them sharp. Tease the top corners at either side of the zip to give them an equal (roughly) 45-degree angle and press with a hot iron to complete (see M).

> ## Tip
> When stitching in zips, try working from the centre to one end, then again from the centre to the other end. That way, you can zip or unzip the zip head and not have to stitch past it, which can make your stitch line uneven.

Lace Clutch

Add a touch of glamour to your summer outfits with this simple-to-make yet eye-catching floral lace clutch. Have fun with colours by experimenting with shades from opposite ends of the colour wheel.

You will need

- Two pieces of 15¾in x 11in (40 x 28cm) lace fabric
- Four pieces of 15¾in x 11in (40 x 28cm) orange cotton fabric
- Two pieces of 15¾in x 11in (40 x 28cm) iron-on medium-weight interfacing fabric
- Two pieces of 2 x 1³⁄₁₆in (5 x 3cm) orange cotton fabric for the zip
- Sachet of blue dye
- Salt
- 15¾in (40cm) turquoise zip
- Thread to match fabric
- Sewing machine and zipper foot
- Embroidery thread and needle
- A hardcover book
- Iron and ironing board
- Fabric scissors
- Handkerchief or pressing cloth

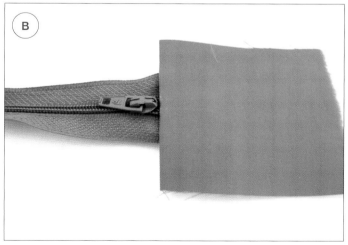

1 First dye the lace fabric panels by following the instructions on the back of the packet and allow to dry (see A). Cover with a damp cloth and carefully iron on the two interfacing fabrics with a medium heat to the reverse of the two orange fabric panels and allow to cool.

2 Place one of the small 2 x 1³⁄₁₆in (5 x 3cm) orange rectangular pieces of fabric at one end of the zip, raw edges together, and sew in place. Fold the fabric away from the zip (see B) and sew vertically to hold in position, repeat the same process at the other end of the zip.

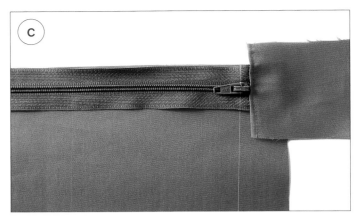

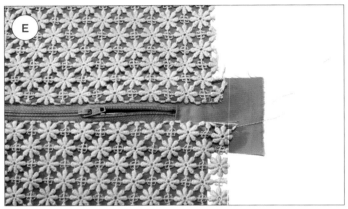

3 Place one liner fabric (the interfaced piece) right side up with the zip on top, making sure the top of the zip is aligned with the top of the fabric (see C). Place a lace fabric panel and a plain orange fabric panel on top of the zip (these two panels form the outer panel of the clutch) and pin in place. Using a zipper foot on your sewing machine, sew along the top edge to sew the layers together (see D).

4 Flip the pieces of fabric you sewed down to the other side of the zip so that you can see the bare side of the zipper, and then place the last liner fabric piece under the zip, right side up. Place the lace fabric panel and the final orange fabric panel over the zip as in Step 3, pin in place and sew the layers into position. Once you have the panels attached, open the piece out, right side up (see E), pin the fabric around the zip and using the zipper foot sew along the edge of the zip.

5 With the zip open, pin the liner fabric pieces right sides together and then the lace and orange outer fabric pieces right sides together. You should have a large rectangle with the zip running across the middle (see F).

6 Sew all the way around the rectangle but leave a 4in (10cm) opening at the base of the lining end, backstitch either end. Trim the corners and any extra fabric at the zip ends, and then push the bag out through the opening, making sure you poke the corners out with the tip of the scissors. Tuck in the raw edges of the opening and sew shut with a running stitch. Fasten off any stray threads then finally put the lining back inside the bag.

Tips

Pin a length of wide webbing folded in half inside the bag so that the raw ends are aligned with the bag edge at Step 6, if you prefer a strap.

Take your time when sewing through the layers and the zip.

Have fun with colours by thinking about shades from opposite ends of the colour wheel.

7 To make the tassel, find a hardcover book that is as wide as you want the tassel to be in length. Wrap the embroidery thread around the book widthways about 20 times (see G). Cut three pieces of thread about three times the length you want the hanger string to be, slip all three underneath the wrapped yarn and tie in a strong knot.

8 Braid the six ends (two in each portion) together to form a plait and then tie a knot at the end. At the opposite end of the book, cut the wrapped thread; this will separate the tassel from the book. To form the rounded top and the skirt of the tassel, take a long length of the thread, tie it around the tassel about 1in (2.5cm) from the top and turn so that the thread wraps around to form a thick cinch. Tie in and neaten off. Trim off the messy ends to give the tassel a nice thick skirt and then attach it to the zip (see H).

Evening Bag

This elegant evening bag is full of vintage charm and understated glamour. Browse online or in your local thrift shop to source fabric and jewellery for putting together your own unique design.

You will need:

- Pattern templates on page 119
- Photocopier
- Fabric scissors
- 11¾in (30cm) fabric
- 11¾in (30m) lining fabric
- 11¾in (30cm) lightweight wadding
- 8in (20cm) heavyweight interfacing
- Needle
- Thread to match fabric
- Fabric scissors
- Sewing machine and thread
- Iron and ironing board
- Handkerchief or pressing cloth
- Tape measure
- Ruler
- One buckle/brooch
- One large popper

1 Scale up the pattern pieces on page 119 by 250% on a photocopier.

2 Using tailor's tacks, mark the pleats. Tack the wadding around the edge to the wrong side of the bag fabric.

3 With right sides together, fold the fabric in half along its length and, leaving a ⅜in (1cm) seam allowance, tack and machine sew the side seams of the bag fabric and then the bag lining (see A).

4 Open out the side seams and press gently. Then, ¾in (2cm) away from the point at the base of the bag, sew across the seam. This will give the bag a flat base. Repeat on the lining (see B).

5 Place the lining inside the bag, wrong sides together, and tack all three layers together around the top edge. Stay stitch the pleats together 3in (75mm) from the top edge. Put this to one side.

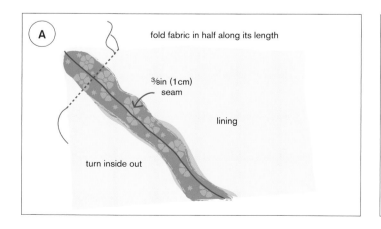

A — fold fabric in half along its length
⅜in (1cm) seam
lining
turn inside out

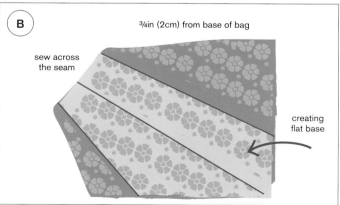

B — ¾in (2cm) from base of bag
sew across the seam
creating flat base

6 Bow: With right sides together, tack and machine along the long edges to make a tube. Turn inside out and press.

7 Handle: Cover with a damp cloth and iron the interfacing onto the wrong side of the handle fabric. Press under a ⅜in (1cm) hem along the long edges (wrong sides together) and then fold the handle in half along the length and topstitch along each edge.

8 Band: Trim ⅜in (1cm) off each edge of the band interfacing and iron onto the wrong side of the four band pieces.

9 If you are using a buckle, slip it onto the bow now and tack the short edges of the bow to the short edges of one of the band pieces. If using a brooch it will be attached later and the bow will seem slightly long for the band when tacked into position; this is to allow for the bow to ruche when the brooch is pinned on.

10 With right sides together, tack and machine two of the band pieces together along the short edges. Now repeat with the other two pieces.

11 Place one of the band tubes inside the other one with right sides together, matching the side seams. At each side seam place each end of the handle with the raw edge in line with the top of the seam and the handle hanging down between the right sides. Tack and machine sew around the top. Turn out and press.

12 Pin the right side of the band (with the bow on it) to the right side of the bag, matching the side seams. Leave the inside of the band free – this will be hand-stitched into place later.

13 Machine sew around the top, turn out and press, then slip-stitch the band facing into position. Lastly, sew the popper pieces to either side of the bag, facing in the middle to close the bag.

Tips

If using striped fabric, remember to match the stripes where possible.

Place your favourite bit of the fabric on the centre front of the bag.

Templates

Bow-trimmed clutch (p13)

Photocopy the bag front and bag back at 110%
Photocopy the bow at 200%

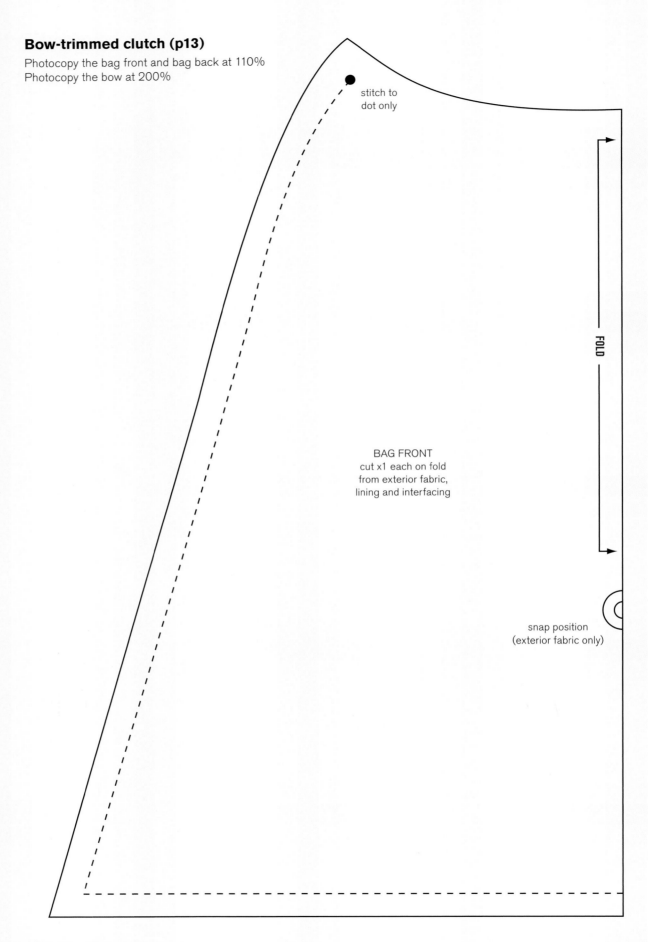

stitch to
dot only

FOLD

BAG FRONT
cut x1 each on fold
from exterior fabric,
lining and interfacing

snap position
(exterior fabric only)

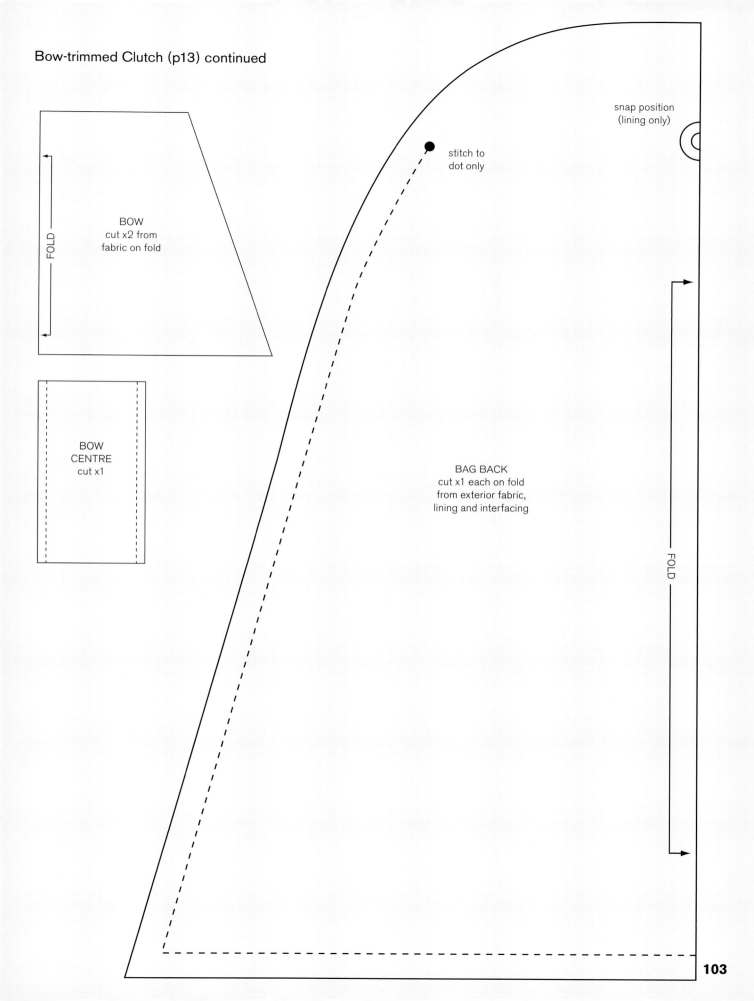

FOLD

BOW
cut x2 from
fabric on fold

BOW
CENTRE
cut x1

stitch to
dot only

snap position
(lining only)

BAG BACK
cut x1 each on fold
from exterior fabric,
lining and interfacing

FOLD

Retro Handbag (p17)

Photocopy at 160%

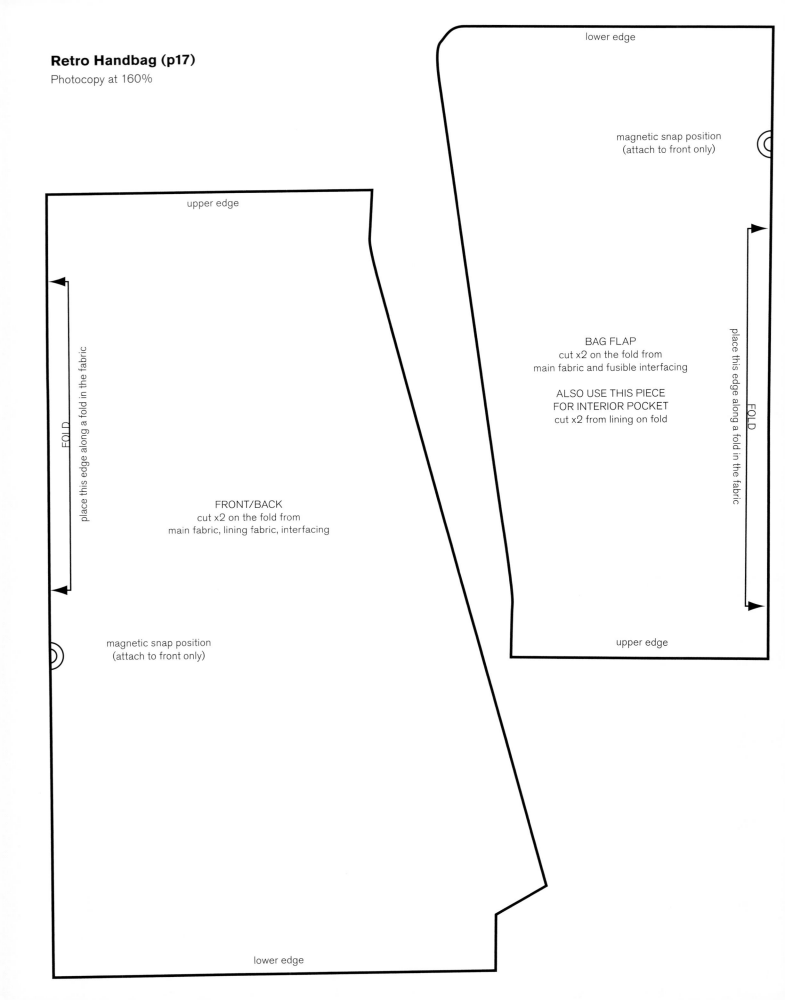

lower edge

magnetic snap position
(attach to front only)

upper edge

place this edge along a fold in the fabric

FOLD

place this edge along a fold in the fabric

FOLD

BAG FLAP
cut x2 on the fold from
main fabric and fusible interfacing

ALSO USE THIS PIECE
FOR INTERIOR POCKET
cut x2 from lining on fold

FRONT/BACK
cut x2 on the fold from
main fabric, lining fabric, interfacing

upper edge

magnetic snap position
(attach to front only)

lower edge

Messenger Bag (p23)

Photocopy as follows:
Flap template at 200%
Front, back and interior pocket template at 200%
Front/back template at 141%

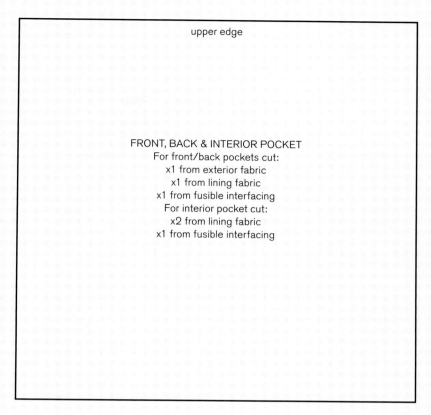

upper edge

FRONT, BACK & INTERIOR POCKET
For front/back pockets cut:
x1 from exterior fabric
x1 from lining fabric
x1 from fusible interfacing
For interior pocket cut:
x2 from lining fabric
x1 from fusible interfacing

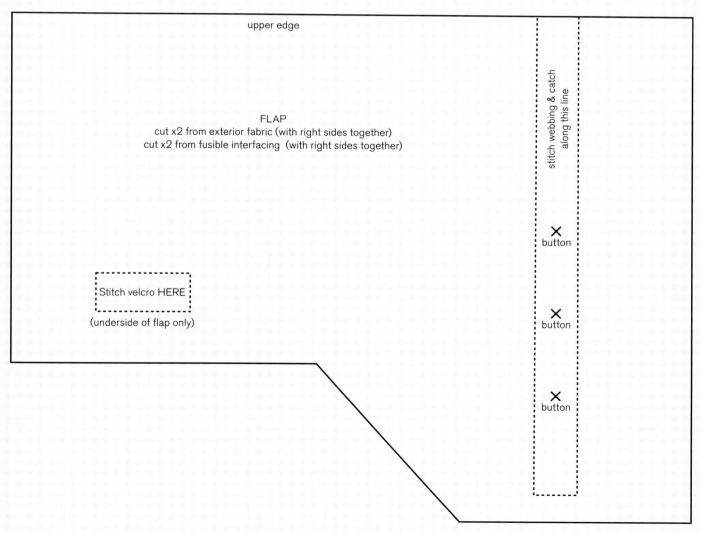

upper edge

FLAP
cut x2 from exterior fabric (with right sides together)
cut x2 from fusible interfacing (with right sides together)

stitch webbing & catch
along this line

✕
button

✕
button

✕
button

Stitch velcro HERE

(underside of flap only)

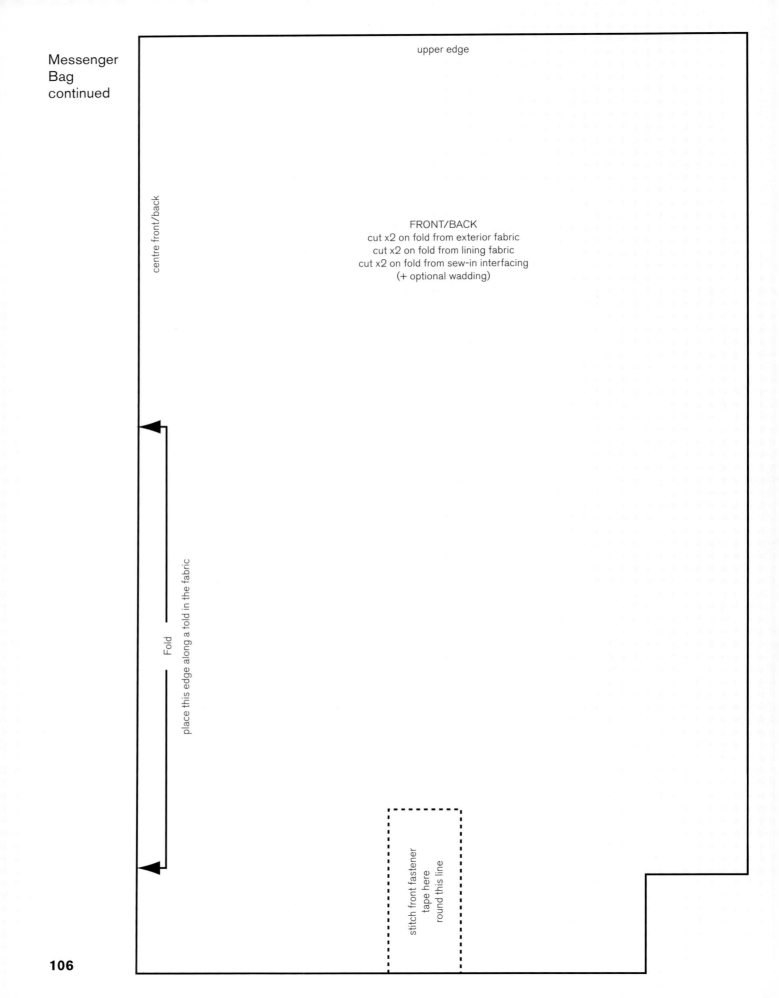

upper edge

centre front/back

FRONT/BACK
cut x2 on fold from exterior fabric
cut x2 on fold from lining fabric
cut x2 on fold from sew-in interfacing
(+ optional wadding)

Fold

place this edge along a fold in the fabric

stitch front fastener
tape here
round this line

Knot Bags (p29)

Photocopy small bag template at 155%
Photocopy shoulder bag templates at 200% and join the pieces
at the dotted line before use (refer to diagram)
Photocopy cross-body bag templates at 250% and join the pieces
at the dotted line before use (refer to diagram)

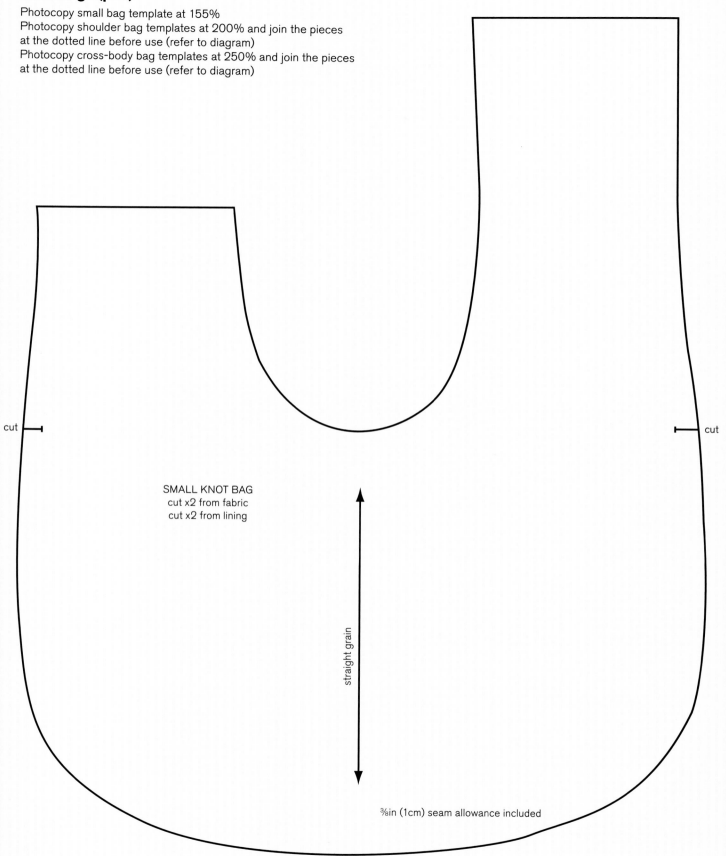

cut

cut

SMALL KNOT BAG
cut x2 from fabric
cut x2 from lining

straight grain

⅜in (1cm) seam allowance included

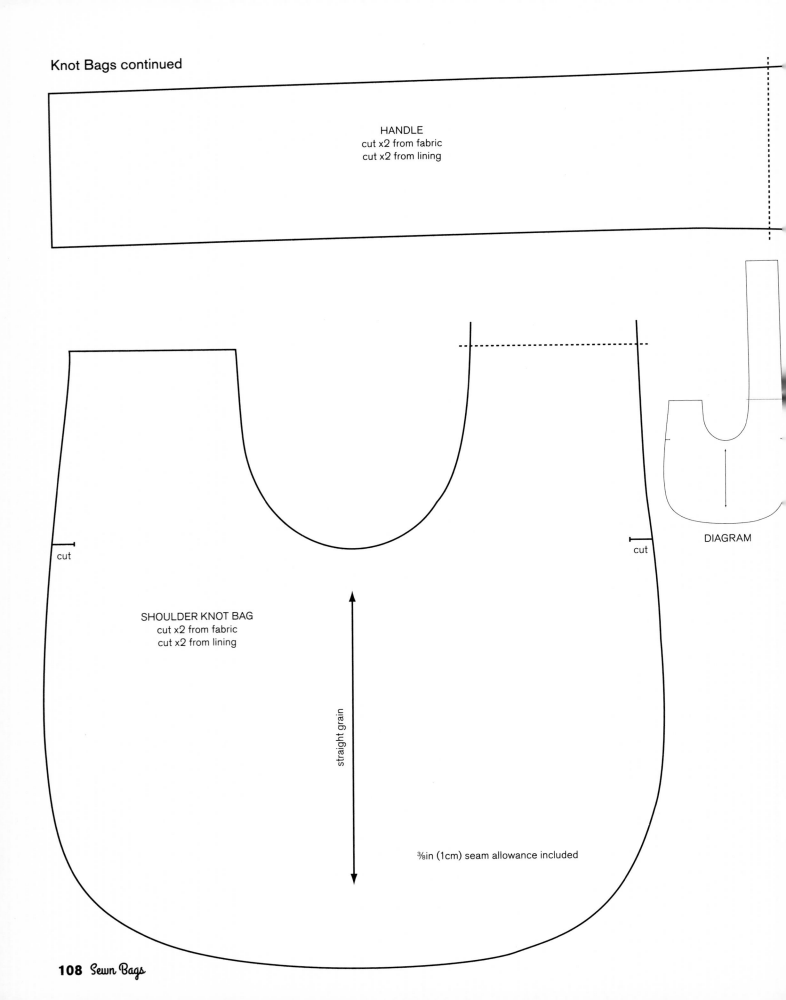

HANDLE
cut x2 from fabric
cut x2 from lining

cut

cut

DIAGRAM

SHOULDER KNOT BAG
cut x2 from fabric
cut x2 from lining

straight grain

⅜in (1cm) seam allowance included

Knot Bags continued

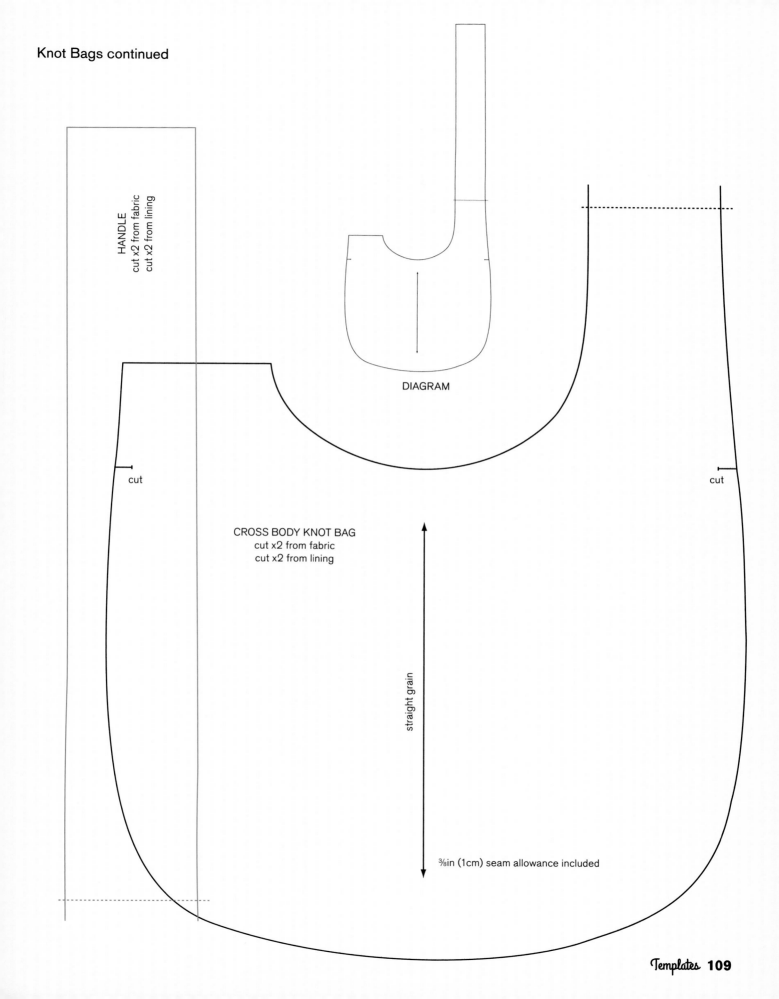

HANDLE
cut x2 from fabric
cut x2 from lining

DIAGRAM

cut

cut

CROSS BODY KNOT BAG
cut x2 from fabric
cut x2 from lining

straight grain

⅜in (1cm) seam allowance included

Stylish Shoppers (p33)

Photocopy at 250%

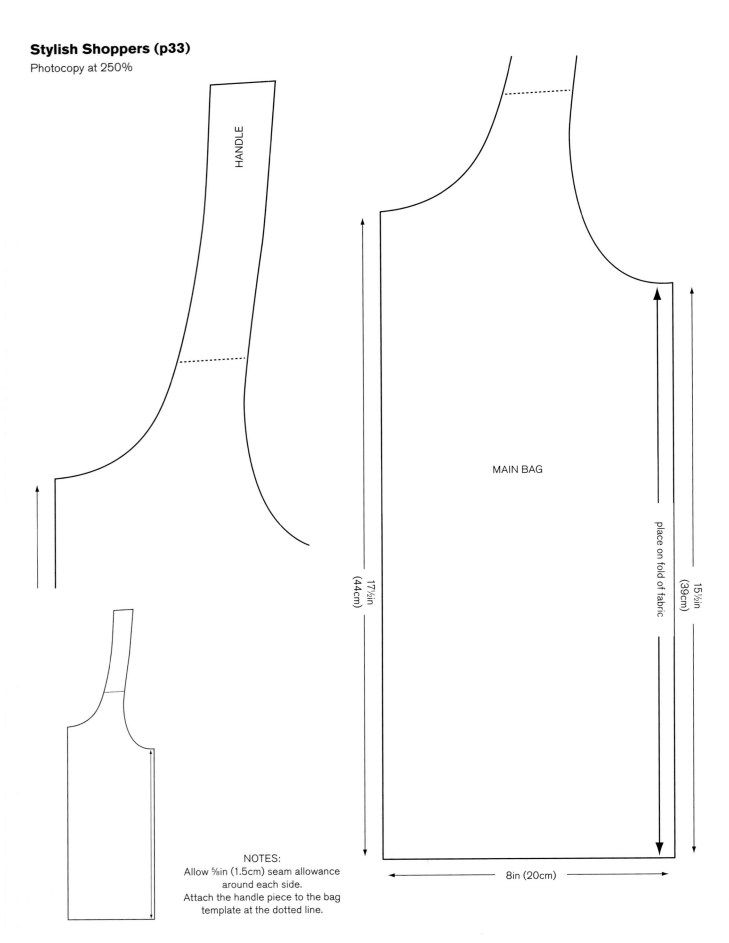

HANDLE

MAIN BAG

17½in
(44cm)

place on fold of fabric

15½in
(39cm)

8in (20cm)

NOTES:
Allow ⅝in (1.5cm) seam allowance
around each side.
Attach the handle piece to the bag
template at the dotted line.

Festival Bag (p41)

Photocopy at 400%

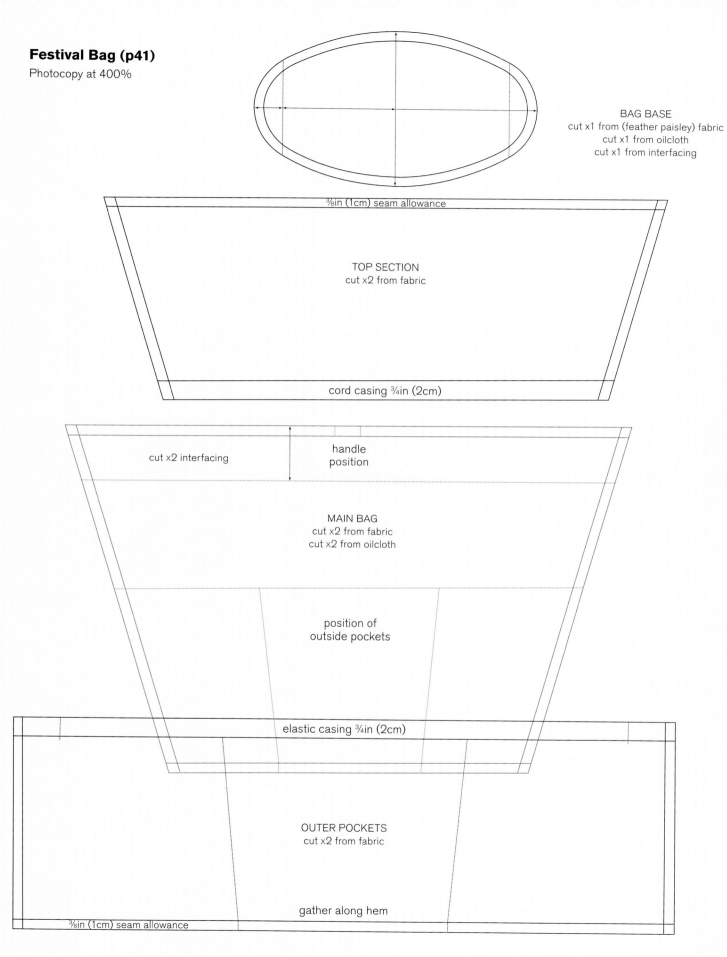

BAG BASE
cut x1 from (feather paisley) fabric
cut x1 from oilcloth
cut x1 from interfacing

⅜in (1cm) seam allowance

TOP SECTION
cut x2 from fabric

cord casing ¾in (2cm)

cut x2 interfacing

handle
position

MAIN BAG
cut x2 from fabric
cut x2 from oilcloth

position of
outside pockets

elastic casing ¾in (2cm)

OUTER POCKETS
cut x2 from fabric

gather along hem

⅜in (1cm) seam allowance

Slouch Bag (p45)

Photocopy at 280%

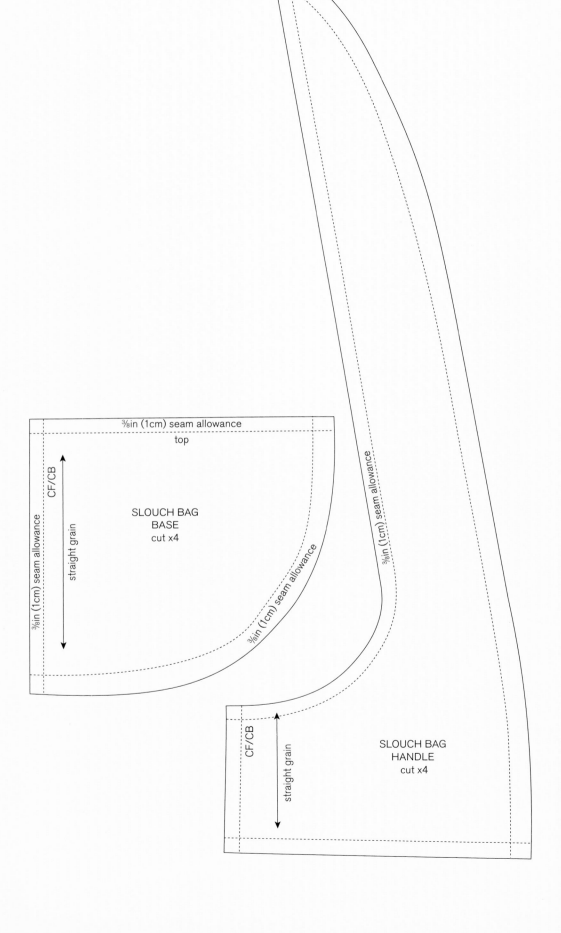

⅜in (1cm) seam allowance

top

CF/CB

⅜in (1cm) seam allowance

straight grain

SLOUCH BAG
BASE
cut x4

⅜in (1cm) seam allowance

⅜in (1cm) seam allowance

CF/CB

straight grain

SLOUCH BAG
HANDLE
cut x4

Gabardine Backpack (p49)

Photocopy at 432%

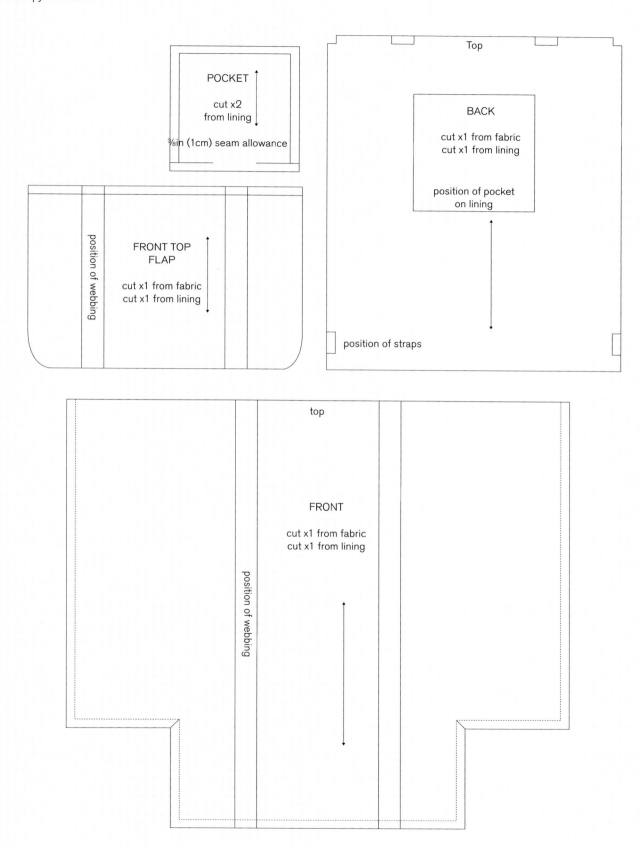

POCKET

cut x2
from lining

⅜in (1cm) seam allowance

FRONT TOP
FLAP

cut x1 from fabric
cut x1 from lining

position of webbing

Top

BACK

cut x1 from fabric
cut x1 from lining

position of pocket
on lining

position of straps

top

FRONT

cut x1 from fabric
cut x1 from lining

position of webbing

Pretty Tote (p53)

Photocopy at 250%
(all pieces include ⅜in (1cm) seam allowance)

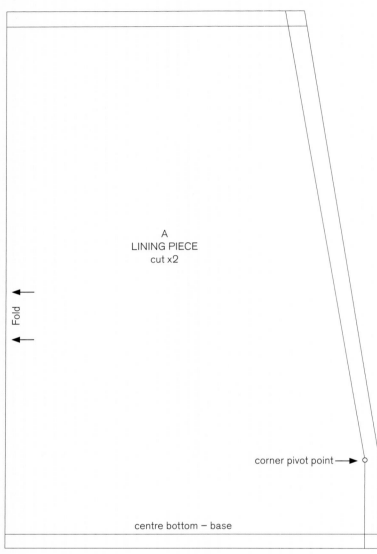

A
LINING PIECE
cut x2

Fold

corner pivot point ➝ ○

centre bottom – base

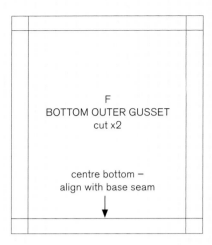

F
BOTTOM OUTER GUSSET
cut x2

centre bottom –
align with base seam
⬇

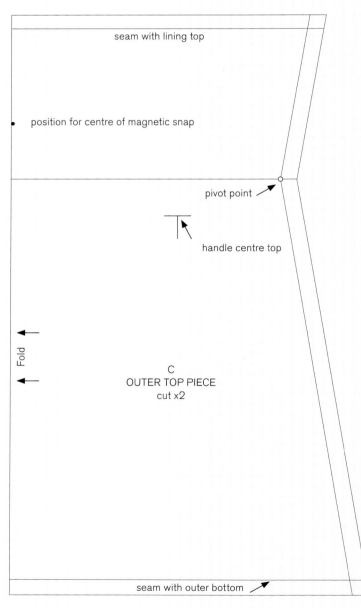

seam with lining top

• position for centre of magnetic snap

pivot point ➝ ○

handle centre top

Fold

C
OUTER TOP PIECE
cut x2

seam with outer bottom ➝

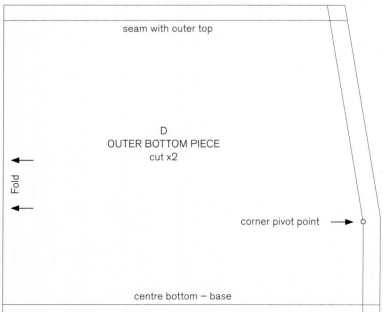

seam with outer top

D
OUTER BOTTOM PIECE
cut x2

Fold

corner pivot point ➝ ○

centre bottom – base

Pretty Tote continued

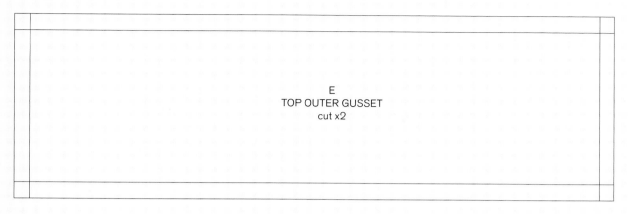

E
TOP OUTER GUSSET
cut x2

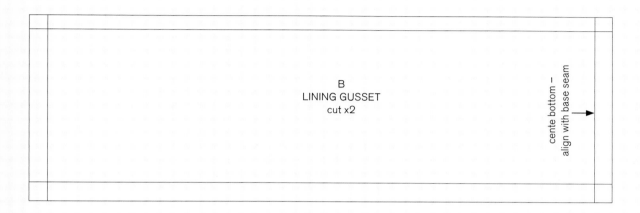

B
LINING GUSSET
cut x2

cente bottom –
align with base seam →

Patchwork Holdall (p57)

Diagram layout

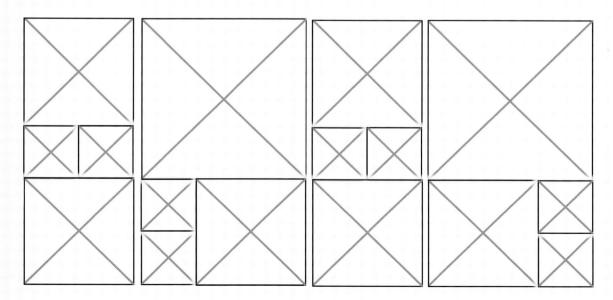

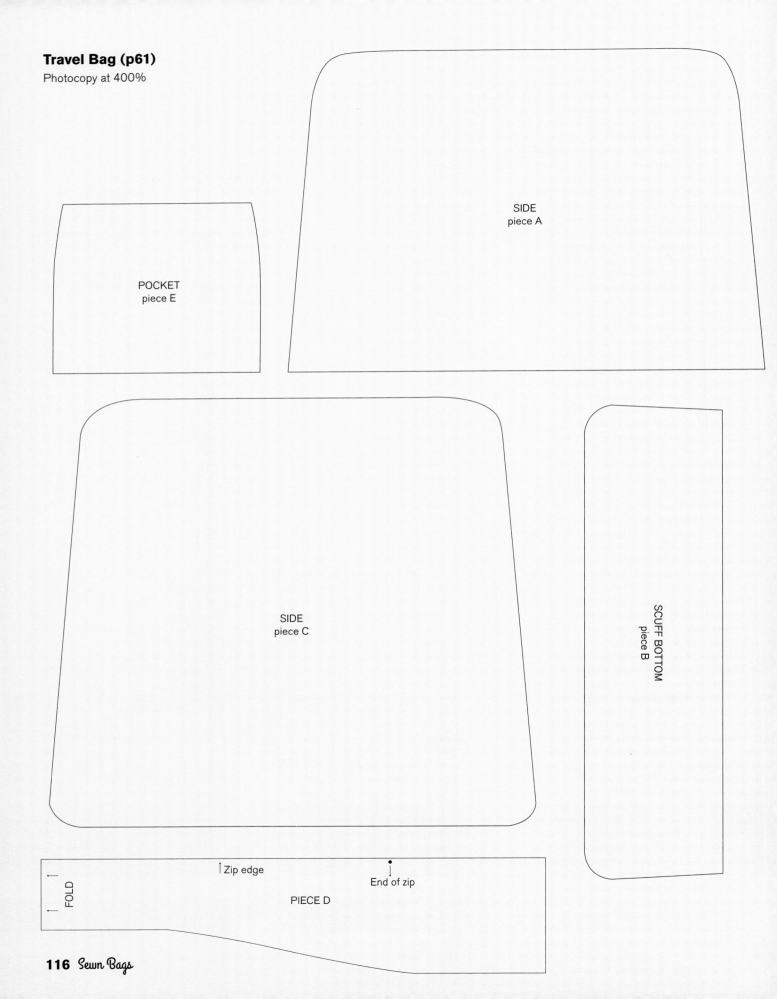

Travel Bag (p61)
Photocopy at 400%

SIDE
piece A

POCKET
piece E

SIDE
piece C

SCUFF BOTTOM
piece B

Zip edge

End of zip

FOLD

PIECE D

BASE
piece F
cut x1 each from plain fabric,
lining and fusible stabilizer

Embellished Bag (p83)

Photocopy at 250%

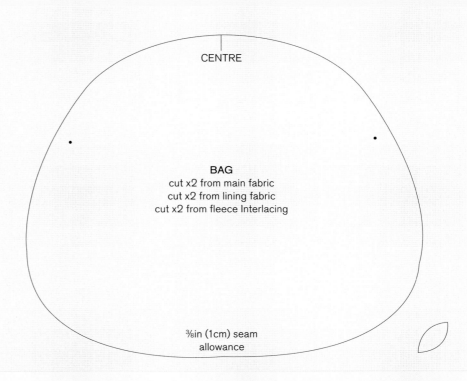

CENTRE

BAG
cut x2 from main fabric
cut x2 from lining fabric
cut x2 from fleece Interlacing

⅜in (1cm) seam
allowance

Felted Bag (p73)

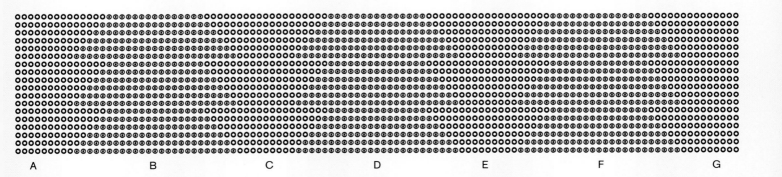

A   B   C   D   E   F   G

**Reversible Shopper
(p79)**

Photocopy at 200%

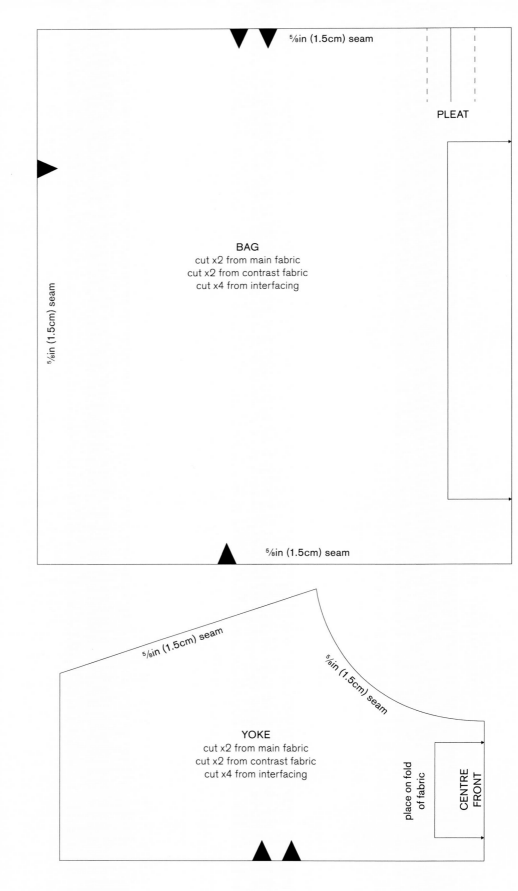

⁵⁄₈in (1.5cm) seam

PLEAT

BAG
cut x2 from main fabric
cut x2 from contrast fabric
cut x4 from interfacing

⁵⁄₈in (1.5cm) seam

⁵⁄₈in (1.5cm) seam

⁵⁄₈in (1.5cm) seam

⁵⁄₈in (1.5cm) seam

YOKE
cut x2 from main fabric
cut x2 from contrast fabric
cut x4 from interfacing

place on fold
of fabric

CENTRE
FRONT